I0186385

Arise from the Ashes

ARISE FROM THE ASHES

An Anthology of Stories

Paulette Harper

Thy Word Publishing
California

Published by Thy Word Publishing
Antioch, CA 94531

Arise From The Ashes
© 2018 Paulette Harper

All rights reserved. No part of this book may be used or reproduced, stored in or introduced into a retrieval system, or transmitted in any form including, photocopying, electronic or mechanical, recording or by any means without the express written consent from the author.

Scripture quotations marked "NKJV" are taken from the New King James Version. Copyright © 1982 by Thomas Nelson, Inc. Used by permission. All rights reserved.

Scripture quotations marked "KJV" are taken from the Holy Bible, King James Version, Cambridge, 1769. Used by permission.

Scripture quotations marked (NIV) are taken from the Holy Bible, New International Version®, NIV®. Copyright © 1973, 1978, 1984, 2011 by Biblica, Inc.™ Used by permission of Zondervan. All rights reserved worldwide.

Scripture quotations marked (NLT) are taken from the Holy Bible, New Living Translation, copyright ©1996, 2004,

2015 by Tyndale House Foundation. Used by permission of Tyndale House Publishers, Inc., Carol Stream, Illinois 60188. All rights reserved.

Arise From The Ashes
Paulette Harper
paulette@pauletteharper.com
Author Website: www.pauletteharper.com

Library of Congress Cataloging-in-Publication Data

ISBN-13: 978-0-9899691-9-2
ISBN-10: 0-9899691-9-3

Published and printed in the United States of America.

Contents

Losing To Win

 ❧

Paulette Harper

"Never Let Disappointments in Life Define Your Purpose"

This was the moment that would change my life forever. There was no turning back, no second guessing my decision, and no one saying let's begin again. It was the day I decided to file for divorce. The life I'd wanted, prayed for, and even moved a thousand miles to get, was not the life it turned out to be. There were no signs, no red flags, nothing to forewarn this marriage was not God's best for my life. It appeared good, but one lesson I learned: good was not enough. I wanted more, I needed more, I deserved more. After all, I belonged to God, and I knew He only wanted the best for my life.

When I said *yes* to the marriage proposal, I knew exactly what it meant. Packing up my belongings and shipping all my things to another state. It meant building new relationships and going to a place that was unfamiliar. When you're in love, distance doesn't matter, especially when—at that point in your life—you never considered the what ifs. What if this marriage didn't work? Who goes into a marriage with a second plan? I sure didn't.

It was the most heartbreaking decision I had to make, but I knew my emotional, spiritual, and mental health hung in the balance. I had to ask myself these hard questions. Could I emotionally continue on this path that didn't appear as if it was headed into greener pastures? Would I allow my spiritual condition to suffer at the hands of another? Mentally, would I accept that the life I was living was beneath its full potential? When you realize maybe you are living beneath your full potential, you will make big moves.

So with that, I resigned myself to the fact my marriage was over, and this chapter in my life was not going to have a happily-ever-after ending.

It wasn't easy to accept, but it was a decision that forced me to reassess my life and what I wanted from it. I. Wanted. Happy! And that meant returning to California to start a new chapter.

A decision got me there; a decision got me out.

During this transition, I found the strength that only comes from God. "He giveth power to the faint;

and to them that have no might he increased strength. Even the youths shall faint and be weary, and the young men shall utterly fall. But they that wait upon the Lord shall renew their strength; they shall mount up with wings as eagles; they shall run, and not be weary; and they shall walk, and not faint" (Isaiah 40:29-31, KJV).

It was in this place the only thing that made any sense was God's promises. "We are assured and know that [God being a partner in their labor] all things work together and are [fitting into a plan] for good to and for those who love God and are called according to [His] design and purpose" (Romans 8:28, AMPC).

Have you been there? Have you made a decision that left you wondering how in the world am I going to get out of this? I had to admit, I was there, and treading on new terrain, new challenges, and it was very uncomfortable.

In my own eyes, this wasn't the ideal place for me, but it was ideal for God. He never said there wouldn't be bumps on the journey, flats in the road, or even pitfalls that would trip us up. However, He did promise us He would make every crooked path straight.

"And I will bring the blind by a way that they knew not; I will lead them in paths that they have not known: I will make darkness light before them, and crooked things straight. These things will I do unto them, and not forsake them" (Isaiah 42:16, KJV).

On the inside, I was fighting my fears. And in my mind, I was thinking about the things I had lost. Yet, once again, God reminded me of one of His promises. "And Jesus answered and said, Verily I say unto you, there is no man that hath left house, or brethren, or sisters, or father, or mother, or wife, or children, or lands, for my sake, and the gospel's. But he shall receive an hundredfold now in this time, houses, and brethren, and sisters, and mothers, and children, and lands, with persecutions; and in the world to come eternal life" (Mark 10:29-30, KJV).

There was nothing I had lost that God did not have the ability to replace and restore. So what was I fretting about? It's only natural to look at a situation and add up all the bad things that transpired or feel like all the time and money you've invested was in vain. It's only natural to feel you've lost more than you've gained. Those are human emotions that come along with the territory. But just because it's natural to feel one way, it doesn't mean I need to feel that way the rest of my life.

From Sarah Jakes Roberts' book *Don't Settle For Safe:* "This poison that taints our memories of the past didn't just come from the hurt we experienced; it also came from the sacrifices we made to endure those moments. While we strive to take a look back at our history, we may mourn the things we feel we lost. That loss may have been even more extreme than the pain of the hurt."

This statement spoke to my heart. It was exactly how I was feeling. Sure, I was hurt about the divorce, but I was more hurt because of the sacrifices I'd made. I would constantly rehearse in my mind the things I gave up: my job, my apartment, my ministry, and all for naught.

I know there is absolutely nothing in life that has happened that God can't use to restore us. Even me coming back to California empty-handed!

Another lesson I learned is that afflictions, heartaches, and difficulties have a way of highlighting things that matter most in life. The purposes for which God allows them to appear go way beyond just us.

No one said life would not be challenging, and God never promised life would come without disappointments. Challenges and disappointments allow us to reevaluate life, so we can make better choices, reassess what happened wrong and right, and hit the reset button—to start anew. No one knows better than me, for I have hit the reset button many times.

It takes courage to start over, and even more challenging is having a heart filled with optimism. To do both requires a person to be intentional. I have this motto: *Intentionally Living on Purpose.* I didn't realize the true meaning until I was forced to rediscover who I was and what I wanted in life. With the help of the Lord and by His strength, I was determined to live life on my own terms and not settle for anything less than God's best for my life.

Maybe you're at a moment in life where you need to make a decision about your own future. Maybe you've made the decision, but fear and insecurities have filled your head with reasons you shouldn't move forward. Maybe those voices are trying to talk you out of taking that step of faith. Saying such things as, *you can't do it,* or *you don't have the money.* Know this, you are not alone. I've been there so many times throughout my journey. It's those voices I had to confront. It's those voices that might have stopped me from moving forward had I listened to them. Until you confront the negativity, those same voices will keep you in the past and prevent you from embracing your future.

Don't allow past experiences to hinder you from moving into your purpose. Don't allow your past to negatively affect your future. It might be difficult at first, but it's so worth the fight. It's worth the struggle; it's worth the reward.

In these moments, remember you can create the life you deserve and desire. Confront your fears, silence the voices, and make those big moves! Yes, God controls the outcome of our journeys, but He gives us the willpower and fortitude to do the work.

I could have talked myself out of leaving because of money, fear, doubt, and insecurities, but I dared to trust God with the unknown. I took God at His Word. "I'll show up and take care of you as I promised and bring you back home. I know what I'm doing. I have it all planned out—plans to take care of you, not abandon you, plans to give you the future you hope for" (Jeremiah 29:11, MSG).

My decision forced me to create new goals and a new vision for my life. Instead of looking at my situation as a failure or loss, I looked at it as an opportunity to live again. I was determined to use what had happened as a stepping-stone to dispel and defy the odds that were against me. I encourage you to use the disappointments in life, the setbacks, the pain, as stepping-stones to make progress and advancement. God does not want you to become stuck or complacent with life. Take what has happened and use it to propel you to greatness; use it to help push you beyond your own limitations and boundaries. Never let an opportunity pass you by because you are still looking in the rearview mirror.

Believe me, I could have been bitter about the entire situation, but I wasn't. Don't get me wrong. I had plenty of time to process the results of my decision. Divorce was a painfully difficult choice. However, once the decision was made, I had to make plans for my new future. Sometimes what appears as a loss or total devastation is actually a win. But until you see that good can come from it, you'll always wonder if you made the right choice. As difficult as the decision was, I had to believe that God was giving me another fresh start for a brand new beginning. I was starting over fresh, and I gladly embraced the unpredictability life was about to bring.

Removing the Mask

Life can deal some devastating blows. Many times, unexpected things occur without any warning and can take the wind out of your sail. We choose to view our future through past experiences. I know that's what I did. When I returned to California I had a list of dos and don'ts. My list also included the kind of person I wouldn't marry again and the person's occupation. Since I had been down this road before, I was determined to protect myself from another letdown. I remember a friend wanted to introduce me to someone and after she told me all his wonderful qualities, I asked her what his occupation was and she told me he was a pastor. I replied, "No thank you." That experience changed me and my perceptions of what being married to a pastor was like.

God gives us choices in life. He doesn't choose for us but gives us the opportunity to make a decision based on facts. I know all men are not the same—but for me—I just didn't want to repeat this pattern. If it's the will of God for me to be married again, I'll meet someone who loves Jesus, serves in the church, and will dote on me like I deserve. I am more determined to stop this cycle from happening again. I have a history of giving myself to people who fail to see my value. Therefore, I choose to create a new pattern with resolve and move forward.

Before you can truly move on, you must identify those areas that might hinder you from moving forward. Growth occurs when we confront our past experiences and their effect on us. If we pretend all is well, when in reality it's not, a pattern will continue in another relationship and you'll find yourself face to face with that issue again.

What's Growing on Your Tree?

"A good tree cannot bear bad fruit, nor can a bad tree bear good fruit" (Matthew 7:18, NKJV). You cannot have good and bad fruit growing on the same tree. A diseased tree will never have the ability to produce anything other than diseased fruit. A tree that has bad fruit growing on it is unhealthy, worthless, and sick. In verse 19 of Matthew, Chapter 7 it reads, "Every tree that does not bear good fruit is cut down and thrown into the fire."

Jesus must cut away things that are growing on our trees as a result of the pain, sorrows, and disappointments of life. If God allows the bad fruit to continue growing, we will never become healthy from our experiences that He has allowed to come. And

God's desire is for all of us to be healthy and useful and producing good fruit, which brings glory to Him.

The Bad Fruit of Defensiveness

This is an area in my life that I need God to prune. Because I didn't defend myself from the emotional and verbal abuse from previous relationships, I have now put up a guard around my heart. Until God sends me someone I can fully trust not to verbally or emotionally abuse me, this mechanism will be used to block any man who I perceive will hurt me. I need my heart to be open to the possibility that God will send me someone who really knows how to love me.

My. Ugly. Truth. What's yours?

In order to really thrive in life, you must confront the effects the past has had on you. I know it might be painful, but believe me, it's better to speak your truth now before a habit is repeated.

There comes a time in all our lives when we must face issues that make us uncomfortable, issues that are associated with pain. But in order to really embrace the new—those old mindsets, those old behaviors, and those old ideas must be confronted. Accepting the bad moments in life requires us to trust that God will turn every bitter experience sweet. He is able to cause the worst situations, the worst experiences, the hardest conditions, to turn into something that works toward our good.

God is looking at how you react to the changes of life. What people do to you is not His main concern, yet He pays attention. What concerns God is how you react and how you respond.

Maybe you're dealing with shame, regret, rejection, fear, unforgiveness, or maybe you have a problem trusting again. In this new season, it's time to stop hiding your true feelings. A lot of us hide behind how we truly feel. We cover up the pain by smiling, joking, and even saying, "I'm okay." But the truth of the matter is, you're not. Remember faking joy can only last so long. The inner turmoil is bound to come out sooner or later.

Moving on takes courage and must be intentional. In this new season, you must be willing to remove the mask and allow God to heal every part of your life that is a threat to your success. He can gather all the broken pieces and put them back together—not like it was before, but better. The real you is dying to come out and you don't have to put on a disguise anymore.

As long as you have breath to breathe, there is still hope and promises for a better tomorrow. Our bad experiences never leave us with the impression we have won anything. We feel defeated, depleted, and worn out. And totally giving up seems like a better solution. The feeling of loss tries to rob us of our joy, our peace and it tries to stop our momentum.

Especially when the loss seems so enormous. How can you recover from such heartbreak and devastation that leave you feeling paralyzed?

When life's tragedies occur, remember you are much stronger than you realize and you have the ability to bounce back. You can't quit, wave the white flag of surrender, or even stop living. God knows those moments will come. The experiences come through Him first and He allows them to happen. Not to break you, but to use them to empower you. Fix your face, wipe those tears away, get out your planner and start living again. Travel, start that business, get that degree, write that best seller, write that play and watch God do His greatest work when you give Him the opportunity to move.

The choice is yours. Either you'll succumb to the adversity or you'll pick yourself up, dust the effects off, and forge ahead. Remember God got you.

Here's an excerpt from my book, *That Was Then, This Is Now* that ties in well here: "Everything that has happened to us, pleasant and unpleasant, has shaped us to be the people we are today. He will use life's circumstances to redefine your character and bring necessary changes to your person. No matter what life has thrown our way, what blows have come, what road we have taken, the plan of God will always remain. The purpose for which you were created will stand. Destiny is within us."

Fast-forward. Since returning to California, I had

no idea how God was going to restore me. He has blessed me with a new home and a new job. My business is growing, and I'm still writing best sellers and award-winning novels.

Friends, rise up out of that pit of discouragement. Your life is not over! Position yourself and declare that you are taking God at His Word and you are going to break out.

As long as you have breath to breathe, there is still great hope and promise for a better tomorrow. Capture every moment and press your way through. Don't allow a moment to pass you by without making the choice to rise above it all. God is still good, regardless of the circumstances, no matter how severe they may appear at the moment. His goodness will be seen in your life as His grace and His power destroy any bondage that holds you captive. Break forth and shine! You are a carrier of God's favor. Selah.

Decide today that you are coming out—out of depression, out of dejection, out of discouragement, and out of your old way of thinking. There is an open door that God has put before you and choices to make that will transport you from your current miserable state into a place of God-ordained rest.

Regardless of your current condition, there is a better place that God has for you. God takes great pleasure in seeing you happy. You must decide to move forward and allow God to redirect you. Allow

Him to lead you to greener pastures and still waters. Allow Him to restore your soul.

"But thanks be to God, which giveth us the victory through our Lord Jesus Christ."

(1 Corinthians 15:57, KJV).

Losing. To. Win.

About the Author

Behind her smile is a woman who has learned the real meaning of endurance, faith and tenacity. Bestselling, award winning author and marketing specialist, Paulette Harper has authored several books, including her award winning novel *Secret Places Revealed*, and her award winning inspirational book *Completely Whole*.

Her literary works have been spotlighted in a growing number of publications, including CBN, The Sacramento Observer and Real Life, Real Faith Magazine.

As an inspirational speaker, Paulette's presentations are inspiring, enriching and encouraging. Her ability to share and connect with her audience comes from her own life's journey and experiences. She lives her life based on her motto: Intentionally Living Life on Purpose.

Paulette lives in Northern California.

To book Paulette for your next event contact her: paulette@pauletteharper.com

Visit her online: www.pauletteharper.com

Unfailing Love

⁓⧉⁓

Yolando Cooksey

"Turn, Lord, and deliver me; save me because of your unfailing love" (Psalm 6:4, NIV).

4:30 a.m.

I was lying in bed, not sure what day it was or what I'd done the night before. Suddenly the other side of the bed moved. Wait! What's that touching my feet? Is that a hand I feel? I quickly turned over to see a strange man next to me.

"Oh no, not again." I trembled at the thought of another encounter.

I slid my feet to my side of the bed and removed his hand. Luckily he was not fully awake. My head hurt. I felt groggy and the room was spinning. I should have known better than to go partying with the girls last night. I finally remembered it was Saturday morning.

Thank God I didn't have to get up early, and the boys would not be getting up anytime soon.

Thinking of my two sleeping sons shot a familiar pain through my heart. There should have been three boys down the hall. I lost my sweet Shannon at just six weeks old. Crib death, they told me. But, it must have been something I did. Guilt and grief consumed me. I tried to distract myself with drugs, alcohol, and men. Too many men.

And this morning there was a stranger in my bed. I promised myself I would not sleep with another man who I wasn't in love with. I was sick and tired of being the side piece, good enough to sleep with but not wife material. Enough of looking for love in all the wrong places. As I contemplated what to do next, I thought, *Well, he's not going to go away on his own, Yolando.* I gathered up all my courage as the room spun from the alcohol. I didn't want to hurt his feelings. He seemed like a really nice guy, but that's how they all start out.

"Good morning, love." I gently ran my hand up and down his arm.

He slid towards me, rubbing his eyes, and smiling as if he was planning to have a morning tune-up.

"I need you to leave now." I hurried from under the cover and dashed into the bathroom.

"Is it something I said? Did I do anything wrong? I was really feeling you. I thought we hit it off pretty well." He sat on the side of the bed trying to clear his head, looking around for his clothes.

When I peeked my head from behind the bathroom door, I saw them. They were all over the room. *Must have been a wild night.*

After a few minutes, I yelled from the bathroom, "Aren't you dressed yet? My kids will be getting up soon and I don't allow them to see strange men in my bedroom." True, I never let my sons see strange men—men I wasn't dating—in my bedroom, but they weren't actually getting up anytime soon. There was a strange feeling inside of me. I knew that was not the reason I needed him to leave. As I came out of the bathroom in my robe, he looked at me with bewildered eyes, wondering what in the world just happened.

"You still not ready?"

He rushed to put on the rest of his clothes. "I'm confused. I really liked you and don't understand why you're kicking me out."

"My bad. I'm sorry." Even though I really wasn't. "I had a nice evening, but like all good things, this must come to an end." I again assured him he had done nothing wrong, he just had to go. I walked him to the door, thanked him for a good time and bid him goodbye.

I flopped back on my bed, wondering what in the world was wrong with me. My head throbbed again as I stumbled to the bathroom looking for aspirin, Tylenol, anything that would stop the pain.

I should grab a beer or something to get rid of this

hangover, I thought, as a wave of nausea hit and I knelt before the porcelain throne. This strange feeling wasn't leaving me alone. Maybe if I took a shower I could shake it off and everything would be okay. But it wasn't okay. I wasn't okay. I found Tylenol, swallowed a couple of them with a glass of water, and crawled back under the covers.

Lying there praying for relief, it dawned on me that I didn't like waking up with strange men in my bed. I didn't like the hangovers, being unable to recall what took place the night before, or how I got home. I didn't like it at all. My life was seriously spinning out of control. Partying, getting high, drinking, passing out, and sleeping with different men was not all it was hyped up to be.

I thought to myself, *What happened to bring me to this place in my life?*

I remembered my first encounter with love. I just knew he was the one. I called my best friend. "Hey, girl, I went on a blind date last night with this guy's brother, and he is fine."

"Go ahead, tell me more."

"He's a light-skinned brother with green or hazel eyes and long hair!"

"He has long hair?"

"Yes, girl, there is something about men with long hair that turns me on. I think I'm in love." I tried to sound sultry.

She knew I had a tendency to fall in love too fast

and needed to slow down. "Girl, it's only been one night. I thought you said you were waiting to find true love."

"I know I said that, but I really think he's the one."

We eventually married and had three sons. We were happy, in love and getting along great until Shannon passed away. Dreaming of Shannon and seeing other babies tormented me day and night, and eventually had a negative effect on our relationship. After ten years of ups and downs, we decided to divorce and go our separate ways. I moved back home with my parents and focused on raising my sons as best I could. Although I was getting used to being a single mom, I still found time to go out with the girls. Shortly afterwards, I was in yet another relationship and again I said, "He's the one." We had dated for about a year and things were going good.

One day I asked him, "Israel, what do you think about our relationship?"

"It's good, babe."

"What would you do if I asked you to marry me? We've been dating for over a year now, and I would like to build a life with you." My eyes examined his face as he looked towards the wall and then looked back at me.

He held his head in his hands, "I don't think that's a good idea. I'm not the marrying kind."

My heart sank to the floor. My emotions were all

over the place. I didn't know if I wanted to slap him, hit him, or kick him.

"Why?"

"I'm not the settling down type."

Running upstairs to my room, I slammed the door behind me. I fell on my bed and sobbed. *How could this be happening again?* I gave him all of me and yet he was not willing to give me all of himself. *Oh, but I was good enough to sleep with.*

"Fine, then I'm going to use men before they use me," I said to myself. I was an angry, hurt, and bitter woman. A wounded woman who did not have hope, did not feel loved, and didn't see a way out.

"This love thing is for the birds, so I'm about to get mine." I stormed out the door. "Be gone when I get home."

It was time for me to concentrate on myself and my sons, NOT a man!

Spiraling downward as the years passed, I couldn't see I wasn't hurting anyone but myself. After numerous relationships looking for "*the one*" to fill the void in my life, the stranger encounter was my rock bottom. The feeling that something wasn't right was God's Spirit awakening inside of me. I remembered scriptures I learned as a child that spoke about God. God is love. He will never leave you nor forsake you. God is not a man that He should lie. He is true to His promises. I decided right then and there, I needed a change. I needed to take a leap of faith and see what God had to offer. I needed to give God a try.

I rolled over onto the floor and began to pray. "Lord, I've tried everything but you. I don't like who I am, who I have become, or who I will be if I continue on this path of destruction. I need you in my life. I'm not sure of what will happen tomorrow, but I know I can't go on without you. Your Word says to test you and see that you are a man of your Word. Lord, I'm tired and I invite you into my heart. I cannot go on like this. Please forgive me. I repent of my sins and confess that I am a sinner in need of a savior, Jesus Christ. Please help me, Lord. In Jesus' name I pray. Amen." At that very moment, I felt a sense of peace, healing, and restoration.

I was now living in Fremont, California, and couldn't wait for Sunday morning.

"Wake up, boys, we are going to church today." I threw the blankets off their beds.

Their eyes still had sleep in them. "Why are we going to church? We haven't been in a while."

"I know, sons. We are starting a new life today."

The boys got dressed while I cooked breakfast. I had been up hours before them, listening to gospel music and praying for God to help me.

I looked in the Yellow Pages for churches in the Fremont area and found Fremont Bible Fellowship. The music lifted my spirits and after the message, I tearfully went to the front of the church and rededicated my life to Christ. I was looking for real love. I needed God's unconditional love to pierce my heart and show me what I had been looking for my entire life.

Like me, many women open themselves up to hurt, pain, rejection, manipulation, and abuse—all because of a need for attention. Often, when hanging out with girlfriends, we exchange our war stories about our experiences with love. We endure physical, mental, and verbal abuse, because we don't see it as abuse, or we are too afraid to leave. We listen to countless negative words spoken into our lives, due to lack of courage to speak up for ourselves. We don't know we deserve to be treated better. The abusive treatment also hurts our children by exposing them to negative behaviors. This is not God's plan for His daughters.

A life-altering change had taken place in me. I acknowledged to God and myself that I could not make it on my own. I was in need of a Savior and I wanted help. I had been looking for love in all the wrong places. I exchanged the love God had for me for a physical love, which only brought me pain. I internalized feelings of low self-esteem, self-worth, and low self-confidence. I did not feel loved after taking a bite of the forbidden fruit, the forbidden fruit of unhappiness and disobedience. I had not only taken a bite, I ate the entire apple without realizing what I had done.

As God's daughters, we were created for love and

to be loved the right way. Genesis 1:27 (NIV) states, "So God created mankind in his own image, in the image of God he created them; male and female he created them." We were not thrown together, wished into existence, or dreamt up. We were created! When an artist creates a painting, time is taken to carefully consider what he or she wants to produce. The artist starts with a blank canvas and visualizes the finished product. The end result is an original masterpiece, not a copy. It has value, character, and in some cases, is priceless. In God's eyesight, we are original masterpieces. We were uniquely designed and created by God and for His purpose. From the beginning of time, God created us for fellowship and relationship with Him first, and then each other. We were created to belong! It is not by accident each of us feels a need to belong to something or someone. Feel that someone really cares about us and cares about what happens to us. Especially as women, we have an innate feeling for connection.

Early one morning while at a conference in Monterey, I decided to go to the beach and talk to God. Wrapped in a blanket and taking off my tennis shoes so as not to get them wet, I stood at the edge of the shore. I looked around as far as I could see to the left and right, seeing nothing but water.

I thought to myself, *How amazing are you, Lord. You created the heavens and earth. You are in control of how far the water comes to the shore before going back out.*

Gazing at how calm the water was, yet realizing the damage it could do when in a storm blew my mind. As I raised both my hands and closed my eyes, I spoke aloud, "I love you, Lord. From my heart I really love you."

When I opened my eyes and looked down, the water was gently lapping my feet as if God was saying, "I Love You, too!"

Now that's love—a love that won't leave your side and is always with you. A love that is unconditional and freely given. I know now I don't have to perform, please, or satisfy anyone else but God. God loves me just because I am His. God feels the same way about you, too. So *Arise from the Ashes*, allow the love of God to flow freely in your life, and experience the true meaning of unfailing love.

About the Author

Yolando Cooksey is a published devotional author in The Upper Room magazine and was recently published in an anthology, The Short and Sweet of It: When the Right Word is a Short Word. She enjoys writing as an expression of sharing her faith and her journey of developing an intimate, personal love relationship with Jesus Christ. Although raised in a Christian home, Yolando did not discover intimacy with God until after suffering several traumatic events in her life. The experiences God allowed Yolando to go through have been her motivation and passion to mentor teen girls and women to find the true meaning of real, authentic, and unfailing love. Yolando's foundation in Christ has been the guiding light in her writing and making a decision to return to school after retiring in 2015. Yolando is pursuing a master's degree in Social Work with a goal to counsel at-risk youth and children in the foster system.

Yolando is a mother, grandmother, friend, and most importantly, a daughter of the Most High God. It is her dream that women truly learn who and whose they are!

Unexpected Life's Transitions

∽⚭∽

Donna Moses

Late one Tuesday evening twenty-eight years ago, I received a phone call from my godsister telling me she needed to talk to me.

She said, "I really can't talk to you on the phone, but I need to come over to discuss this matter in person."

I asked if she would like to come over immediately, and she said she needed to have some quiet time and would definitely see me tomorrow. I knew from this response that she was planning on having an encounter with the Lord before she met with me. By the sound of her voice, I knew she needed me and this wasn't just one of our regular sister talks.

✿

My dear godsister—God's angel—was a beautiful young woman. Energetic, kind, and loving, she followed in her mother's footsteps and became a licensed vocational nurse. She was the sixth child in a family of eight. We both grew up in Indiana and were very close to each other. We continued to bond throughout our childhood, so much so, as adults we became inseparable. She moved from our hometown to join me and my family in California because I had no other relatives living here.

She met the love of her life, and they were united in marriage and had one son together. We spent almost every day together talking about our children, husbands, and just simply sorting out life. A devoted wife and mother, she enjoyed life, working, and going to church.

My mind was running in circles and I found myself thinking about how she had previously been diagnosed with *Non-Hodgkin's lymphoma* at the age of twenty-six. She had experienced night sweats, fever, exhaustion, nausea, chest pain, and coughing. She went through this illness with faith, hope, and strength.

She said, "I have a son and a husband, and I must beat this cancer."

Through God's great love, mercy, and grace, my godsister completed her chemotherapy treatments and radiation.

I was worried that her cancer had returned.

On the next day, I had a prior appointment which I cancelled and waited for her arrival. I paced the floor, not knowing what to expect.

She arrived and flopped on the couch. She said, "I have some news to share with you. My doctor just confirmed that I am pregnant."

I nearly jumped out of my chair and gasped for air because she had been told by her doctor that in no uncertain terms would she be able to get pregnant again. I began to cry and couldn't figure out if these tears were of joy—or fear—for her. She reached out toward me, extending her arms around me, comforting me, and told me she was trusting God for whatever came her way.

About three months into the pregnancy, my godsister had trouble breathing. Her primary care physician made an appointment with the cardiologist, Dr. Fox, to evaluate her medical condition. She asked if I would go with her and I immediately agreed. We arrived at the cardiologist's office where he introduced himself and proceeded to ask a series of questions. Then he examined her. Dr. Fox told her that as a result of her chemotherapy treatment, she had developed *cardiomyopathy*, a progressive disease of the myocardium, or heart muscle. She asked if the disease would affect her pregnancy, and if she would be able to carry her baby full term. Dr. Fox told her that she would be able to without any risks or complications that would be life-threatening. In spite of it all, my godsister was a fighter and a prayer warrior. I knew intuitively she had sought the Lord, and He answered her, and had delivered her from all fear. She and her husband received the news and were so thankful she wasn't in a situation where she would have to choose her life over the life of her child. Newly married with one son, I just knew she had it all together and her challenges with her health were all behind her.

When she was five months along, she began to experience signs of fatigue and as the weeks went on she presented shortness of breath, heart palpitations, and weakness. At twenty weeks she found out the sex of her unborn child—a girl. Dr. Fox immediately put her on bed rest because of the shortness of breath, extreme weakness, and chest pain. The doctor spoke to her husband and requested he ask his wife to consider having an abortion due to presenting complications. He spoke to her just as the doctor had asked. Shouting loudly, you could hear her all through the house, "I refuse. This is my body and *my* choice. I will deliver a beautiful baby girl." Her faith in God was so strong, nothing was going to convince her to doubt Him. She already knew in her mind and heart she wasn't going to make the decision of having an abortion.

I was totally shocked over the news. It just didn't make sense to me that she could be stricken with such a life-threatening condition at such a young age. I was frustrated, and I often thought, *How could God put this battle of sickness and disappointment upon her?* Our mothers always told us we could do all things through Christ who strengthens us (Philippians 4:13, KJV). She seemed to hold on to this scripture and I seemed to waver with questioning God. I could only support my godsister and her husband with love and accept their decision. She had to have a cesarean section before her due date because of her life-threatening condition, putting her and her baby at risk. What an ecstatic and loving moment the two expressed, embracing their baby together.

She had some touch and go moments after her cesarean delivery: extreme weakness, shortness of breath, and an irregular heartbeat, that were frightening. After many weeks, she became stabilized and was discharged to go home without her precious daughter. Being born premature, her daughter needed to stay in the hospital's neonatal intensive care unit until she became stable. She was being monitored for jaundice and apnea, and her weight had to meet a certain criterion before being discharged from the hospital.

My godsister came home from the hospital, still experiencing severe weakness and trying to take in what Dr. Fox had told her before she was discharged. He had explained to her and her husband she was living on what they called *borrowed time,* and she was in the final stages of congestive heart failure.

She asked, "Please explain what you mean, Dr. Fox. What has caused this, and can it be corrected?"

He told her, "Unfortunately, the chemotherapy drug destroyed your heart and it is getting weaker and will completely stop. I can't tell you when it will happen, but I want you to know it could be in a few days to a few months. Please understand that you will need help at home and help with your baby and your other child."

Tears rolled down her face and she asked, "Lord, can you hear me? I am okay with what my life journey has given me. You have blessed me and given me two beautiful children and a wonderful husband. What more could I ask for?" I went to visit my godsister, and we had a long conversation about what she had been thinking. All she wanted was to spend every moment and hour with her baby, son, and husband. I noticed that she was very weak, and short of breath with almost every step she took. I notified her doctor and he had her admitted to Lodi Memorial Hospital. This stay was for two weeks. Her doctor spoke to a physician at Stanford University Medical Center to request a re-evaluation of her. The Medical Center agreed and performed a work-up on her. Their medical team had the same diagnosis. There was nothing more they could do for her. She was transferred back to Lodi Memorial Hospital.

She told her husband, "I am more worried about you than the children."

He said, "I love you, and I love the children, and we will be okay."

Even though he assured her, she asked me to please look after the children and be a mother to them. I was stressed but assured her that I would. She asked her husband if he remembered the Bible scripture from Joshua 1:9 (NIV), "Have I not commanded you? Be strong and courageous. Do not be afraid; do not be discouraged, for the Lord your God will be with you wherever you go." My husband and her husband were present. She told them she felt she had done what the Lord had asked of her and that was to trust Him along the way. She thanked the Lord for His amazing love and she closed her eyes. Her vital signs went flat.

I was devastated, heartbroken, and wasn't prepared for such a loss in my life. I remember telling her mother just like it was yesterday that my godsister, her daughter, had passed. Her mother yelled out a loud scream, "My daughter. Oh my God, my daughter is gone." Her mother relied upon her faith and continued to encourage me, knowing our relationship. I felt as if I might have disappointed her mother and wasn't able to support her like she may have needed. Disconnected from God, I had become bitter and frightened about what was to come. I just couldn't understand my godsister's strength and the peace she'd found. I truly wanted some of that peace to rest upon me. I knew that my life would soon change; I wouldn't have that love and bond we had as godsisters. I had to help my godsister's husband with making arrangements for her home-going celebration. How would we explain this to her son? Her husband was completely lost and relied upon my family for support. This was such a tragedy for our family. Being an adult, you never think of losing someone who is just like a family member to you.

Life was beginning to seem very stressful for me. I was living life without a purpose, still with sadness. It was really hard for me to know that God was real. All I could think of was: Why did the Lord let this happen? I just wasn't ready to redo life without a warning. I wasn't like my godsister—God's angel—who, without a doubt, dialed His number on everything. I was thinking I had my life together, and nothing was going to have my life spinning out of control. My days were spent taking care of my family. Now, I was a full-time aunt to my god-niece of two months, and also an appointed mother to her without a warning. I took responsibility for my god-niece as if I had given birth to her. Loving her, there wasn't anything I wouldn't do for her and her brother.

I was even trying hard to support her husband. He seemed to be in denial and was acting as though she was still alive. He would take the kids—unexpectedly—back and forth from my house, to his house, then to his sister's house. Trying to deal with his emotions was quite challenging and led to my resenting him. My family and I would now have an extended responsibility of caring for a newborn, my god-niece; her brother; and their father. I was working and trying to go back to school. I just knew nothing would get in the way of how I'd planned my life with my family. But it did. Depressed and selfish, I went on with life, not wanting anything to change. My husband was very accepting in this life-changing situation.

My day would begin waking up and being overwhelmed with my added responsibilities. I found it increasing hard to focus on my daily activities. All I could think about was my dear godsister—God's angel. I knew she would have done just what I was doing, and more. All in the name of the Lord, whom she always depended upon. Simply, I was in denial for almost a year following her death. I told my husband sometimes in life an unexpected life's transition occurs that fractures us, leaving us broken. That was how I felt at that time. My husband knew I was struggling with my godsister's death. He suggested I take a bereavement class on death and dying at Kaiser Permanente. I was really glad I took the class. Afterwards, I realized that grief isn't a straight line, but rather a series of curves. A book that was suggested in class explained the five stages that we go through when we are grieving: denial, bargaining, anger, depression, and acceptance. The book teaches the grief process one may go through, but not necessarily in the exact order. I seemed to have experienced all five stages, and sometimes felt I had experienced several at the same time. During some of the different stages, I guess you could say I was in the desert. Just like the Israelites, doubting and not trusting God. Grief has a tendency to creep up on you in the odd hours of the day and night.

I can remember how I really wanted to step in and do the right thing by my dear godsister's children. I seemed to have been looking for a way to manage it all with love. My godsister was my confidant and we shared everything with one another. We would stay on the phone, just listening to each other and having some real down to earth conversations about our children and what their futures might hold for them. We would also have discussions about our husbands and our jobs. One day I had a quiet moment and could hear my godsister's voice ringing loud and clear with these words: "Trust in the Lord with all your heart and lean not on your own understanding; in all your ways submit to him, and he will make your paths straight" (Proverbs 3:5-6, NIV). I began to think about how she always wanted to please God and included Him in everything. In every conversation she would say, "If it is the Lord's will."

I began to realize that I needed more to help me overcome my struggles. The death was truly a battle for me; it wasn't for me to endure by myself. My son saw me crying and asked, "Mom, can we go back to church one day? Maybe God can help you feel better." This touched my heart. I realized that he, too, could see I was sad and that God wasn't a part of my daily life plan. I thought about what he said and began going to church. I knew the Lord, and I believed. My father was a minister, and my mother loved the Lord and shared God's Word with me. It was instilled in me as a child to study the Bible, attend church, and pray. I used to say all the time the best thing my parents did for me was introduce me to Christ.

I was looking for the world to rescue me from my depression and sorrow. I just wasn't finding it out there. But God had a rescue plan for me already in store. God had never left me, nor had He forsaken me. God allowed me to partner with my dear godsister on her journey. I was able to bear witness as she walked through faith and not by sight. She also embraced the fruit of the Holy Spirit: love, joy, peace, forbearance, kindness, goodness, faithfulness, gentleness, and self-control. On this journey, little did I know at the time she was depositing precious spiritual nuggets in me that I could pull out later. Praying daily, I soon surrendered to God, calling out His name Jesus. I fell to my knees one day at church and I remember the pastor preaching, "The Battle Is Not Yours, It's Mine." I felt a change had come over me. It wasn't the same after the Holy Spirit landed upon me.

I began to see God's plan and purpose for me. I found this amazing promise in Jeremiah 29:11-13 (KJV), "For I know the thoughts that I think toward you," saith the Lord, "thoughts of peace and not of evil, to give you an expected end. Then ye will call upon me and go and pray to me, and I will hearken to you. And will seek me and find me, when you search for me with all your heart."

It wasn't just for me to go through life thinking I was hopeless in this situation. During this time of grief, I found some inspirational scriptures that helped me. You say: "I can't manage it," but God would say: "And he said, The things which are impossible with men are possible with God" (Luke 18:27, KJV). You say: "I can't go on," but God would say: "And he said unto me, My grace is sufficient for thee: for my strength is made perfect in weakness. Most gladly therefore will I rather glory in my infirmities, that the power of Christ may rest upon me" (2 Corinthians 12:9, KJV). You say: "I'm tired." God says: "Come unto me, all ye that labour and are heavy laden, and I will give you rest" (Matthew 11:28, KJV). You say: "Nobody really loves me." God says:

"A new commandment I give unto you, That ye love one another; as I have loved you, that ye also love one another." (John 13:34, KJV). You say: "It's not worth it." God says: "And God is able to make all grace abound toward you; that ye, always having all sufficiency in all things, may abound to every good work:" (2 Corinthians 9:8, KJV). You say: "I'm afraid." God says: "For God hath not given us the spirit of fear; but of power, and of love, and of a sound mind" (1 Timothy 1:7, KJV). You say: "I don't have enough faith." God says: "For I say, through the grace given unto me, to every man that is among you, not to think of himself more highly than he ought to think; but to think soberly, according as God hath dealt to every man the measure of faith" (Romans 12:3, KJV).

I am so thankful I have rekindled my relationship with the Lord, trusting Him and putting Him first. Through this life journey, I have learned to replace my feelings of frustration, anxiety, and resentment with joy and reconciliation. I also know I must practice what the Lord tells us in Matthew 22:36-39 (NIV), "Love the Lord your God with all your heart and with all your soul and with all your mind. This is the first and the greatest commandment. And the second is like it: Love your neighbor as yourself." God equips us for all assignments that He gives to us. I was really blessed to have been put in a situation where I needed to put all my faith and trust in God, and through this it has given me so much love, peace, perseverance, strength and hope.

When I was able to open up my heart totally to my godsister's children and extend my love beyond my own biological children, God did a remarkable thing in me. He put a fire in my heart to continue to reach back and bring other children into my home and that is exactly what I did, along with my husband. We were able to partner with the court system and become foster parents to several children from different cultural backgrounds. My experience in loving others and sharing what the Lord has given me is so rewarding. Knowing that I by myself can't change the world, but as a team with my husband, we would change the world for that one person. We were able to see that the children had permanent placements and we tried to instill the Word of God in them. I hope that one day all of the children God has given to me will also be able to remember that we all belong to God, and we must help one another as God has commanded.

Through the death of my godsister, it has brought a new awareness in me I am most grateful for, and that is the fact that God never stopped loving me while I was lost. He gifted me with her legacy that has left a mark on my life forever. I am thankful to God for the person I have become through divine restoration and that He has allowed me to return to Him. I am also grateful for God's forgiveness and that He would entrust me with many of His children. I found solace in the scripture Philippians 4:6 (NIV), "Do not be anxious about anything, but in every situation, by prayer and petition, with thanksgiving, present your request to God. And the peace of God, which transcends all understanding, will guard your hearts and your minds in Christ Jesus."

About the Author

Donna Moses passion is to pen works that will impact the hearts of readers, leading them to Christ. An avid reader, she founded Sistahs in Conversation & Sistahs in Harmony Christian Book Club.

She is a retired nurse, graduate from Sacramento Theological Seminary And Bible College, and a member of Progressive Community Church. A Links Incorporated member, Donna is also a recipient of the Susan B. Anthony Award for her community involvement.

Donna lives in Northern California with her husband, Raymond. They have four adult children and nine gifted grandchildren.

Not Forgotten:
After the Storm

∽

Cassietta Jefferson

"MY GOD, MY GOD, WHY HAVE YOU FORSAKEN ME?
WHY ARE YOU SO FAR FROM SAVING ME, SO FAR FROM
MY CRIES OF ANGUISH? MY GOD, I CRY OUT BY DAY, BUT
YOU DO NOT ANSWER, BY NIGHT, BUT I FIND NO REST"
(PSALM 22:1-2, NIV).

This scripture was going through my mind while I was lying on the floor of a third floor bathroom. A few weeks earlier I found out I was pregnant. My husband and I were so excited. We told everyone! If there had been such a thing as social media at the time, I would have created a post using a picture of a pair of baby booties and tagged everyone in my family. I'd had my first appointment already and was looking forward to the next one when they would do an ultrasound to ensure everything was progressing well.

That afternoon I was ravenous and indulged in a medium fat burger and fat fries. I'm not sure why I remember that detail, but I remember it feeling like the most delicious burger on the planet. I was full and happy. Content in my job as a patient advocate and team leader for the appointment line at Wilford Hall Hospital, my blended family was beginning to gel, and I was having a baby. Life was good.

I went to the bathroom because baby Jefferson was resting on my bladder, and came out of the stall, still feeling queasy and unsteady. Washing my hands, I gazed at my blurry reflection in the mirror, praying that I would make it down the hall to my office. I knew I wasn't going to make it. Up to this point, I thought when people fainted, they went down hard like a pile of bricks, but it wasn't quite that way for me. I got down on my knees, still holding on to the sink, and slid the rest of the way to the floor. Sweating, I rested my face on the floor. Yes, the public bathroom floor. It felt good and cool. I closed my eyes, hoping that someone would come in and find me. But ... nobody came. I thought I was going to die, lying on the bathroom floor in a nondescript building on Lackland Air Force Base. Just minutes away from a military hospital.

Well, I didn't die. My eyes popped open, and God gave me enough strength to walk back to my office. I got to my desk and slumped into my chair, just before my head went down on the desk top. That's when my coworker in the next cubicle noticed something wasn't right with me; I'm forever grateful to her, as well as the nurse and staff who jumped into action on my behalf. Between them, they laid me on the floor, called an ambulance, then called my husband. That was the last thing I remembered before waking up in the hospital.

I don't recall who told me the baby was gone, but I remember feeling heartbroken and confused. I kept trying to recall what I might have done to cause this. Was it the cups of coffee I drank? Or maybe the glass of wine before I knew I was pregnant? I'd begun exercising and frequently ran up the three flights of stairs to my office. Was that it? When the doctor came into the room, he told me I had an *ectopic pregnancy* that ruptured. I ran my theories by him, but he reassured me none of this was my fault, it's just something that happens. He also told me that although it didn't feel like it, I was lucky. I felt anything *but* lucky. That was until I researched and learned death from a ruptured ectopic pregnancy is the leading cause of death in the first trimester. The rupture can cause internal bleeding which could lead to hypovolemic shock, where there is a sudden and significant drop in a person's blood volume. Once the blood volume becomes too low, the organs begin to shut down and fail.

In my case, I made it to the operating room in time. Medical professionals were able to stop the bleeding, but they weren't able to save my ovary and Fallopian tube. They had to be removed. That was the beginning of my spiral into the abyss.

Every day, I was reminded I'm blessed to be alive. I was aware that God's hand was on my life and I was grateful but couldn't help but feel the loss. The ugly, jagged scar that ran from my navel to my pelvis was—and still is—a daily reminder of what I'd survived. I survived. But, I hadn't healed.

A few years later, my husband received orders to move from Texas to my hometown, Las Vegas. I was thrilled! I would get to be around my family and return to my old stomping ground. I would get the opportunity to raise my family in a familiar place where my footing was more sure and I'd have the support of my mom and my big sister. For the first time in months I was feeling hopeful and looking forward to the future.

"But now, Lord, what do I look for? My hope is in you" (Psalm 39:7, NIV).

Soon after the move, I discovered I was pregnant again. Again, we were excited! During my last follow-up in Texas, the doctor told me that even though I only had one ovary and Fallopian tube, I should have no problems conceiving again. I was glad the doctors were right this time and was looking forward to being a mom—in Vegas, surrounded by my family. We were ecstatic and hopeful, sure that God would allow the baby to be carried to term.

Because of my history, at my first appointment I had an ultrasound. I remember vividly the doctor telling me, "I see a lot of debris in your uterus, and this could be something or nothing." She said I could wait or proceed to the next step in terminating the pregnancy. I desperately wanted to wait and see what God would do. Despite my history, and at times despair, I still had hope. After discussing the matter further, we opted to wait and see what happened. The following week I started bleeding and passing pretty large clots. I had my answer, but I was still in denial.

I was rushed to the hospital, where emergency medical personnel performed my second dilation and curettage. And I was angry! I was angry at God for not keeping the pregnancy. I was angry at my husband for not doing something. But mostly, I was angry at myself for having a defective body. I fell into a depression, but it didn't last long. I stayed in bed the requisite week after the D&C, crying and feeling sorry for myself.

Then, it was up and back to work. We'd just purchased a house, and I didn't have the luxury of staying in my stupor. It was back to the business of my life. But I still hadn't healed.

After our next move, to Honolulu, Hawaii, I was still depressed. I had suffered two horrific losses, but life continued on around me despite my sadness. I was hoping the move would be a fresh start. A reset, so to speak. Even the beauty of the island didn't perk me up much. I enjoyed the weather, the ocean, and the beautiful beaches but couldn't push aside my pain. I realized my irrational anger at my husband, but was still not speaking to God, and I was still disappointed in myself. I couldn't do what women all over the world did every day, while God sat idly by and did nothing to help me keep my baby. Yes, I was still bitter!

We'd been on the island for a while when I received the news my favorite person on the planet—my niece—was dying. She'd been sick for a long time and fought such a courageous fight; but she was tired. I was told to prepare myself, which honestly, I had no idea how to do. I was able to talk to her on the phone and knew I had to get back home immediately. I rearranged my schedule and booked a flight, but it was too little-too late. My niece died while I was in the air, trying to get to her for one last conversation. God and I were just getting back on speaking terms, and I felt as if He'd pulled the rug out from under me ... again. Logically, I understood she was no longer suffering or in any pain. That did little to make me feel better. Barely sleeping and still hurting, despite my smile, it was time to move on. I had bills to pay and a life to get back to. A little sad when I returned to Hawaii, I was hopeful somehow things would come together for me. I enjoyed a free first-class upgrade and privacy for the five hour flight. I took the time to have a conversation that was long overdue. I prayed. I cried. I prayed some more. Then—I listened. Nothing.

Before long I found myself pregnant again. This time we told no one. Inside I was excited and once again, hopeful. And why wouldn't I be? People had been reminding me of Isaiah 61:7 (NIV) for months. It read, "Instead of your shame you will receive a double portion, and instead of disgrace you will rejoice in your inheritance." They told me next time I would have multiple babies, double to make up for the babies the enemy stole from me. Once again I believed God and prayed for a full term pregnancy and couldn't wait until I could share our blessing with everyone.

A family member came into town and we jumped into the car and took a tour of the island. The next day I started bleeding and went to the army hospital's labor and delivery department for a check-up. I was sent for labs over the next week and was told, "Let's wait and see." The next week I went back to follow up on the labs, only to discover my human chorionic gonadotropin (hormone produced by the placenta after implantation) levels were increasing slightly, but not doubling in value as they should have been. The doctor feared another ectopic pregnancy, given my symptoms, and suggested an immediate dilation and curettage. I was devastated.

Later, while my husband went for the car, the nurse wheeled me outside and asked if I was okay. I told her I was fine and gave her what passed for a smile, excusing her from sitting with me making small talk. I remember sitting in the wheelchair, literally thinking, *My God, my God, why have you forsaken me?* I felt totally abandoned by God.

I was advised to stay at home for a few days and given medication for pain: Oxycontin. The first day, my pain level was physical and rated about an eight on a scale of one to ten. After that my pain was completely emotional, and I still took the Oxycontin. It made me sleep, and when I was asleep, I didn't feel any pain. I wasn't sad or depressed; I was numb. I slept through an entire week before I realized what I was doing. It was the first time I prayed in more than a year. I joined a church and sang on the praise team, but my faith was shaken. I was singing from a place of brokenness. God and I were back on speaking terms. Our relationship was strained, and our speaking terms wouldn't last long.

"For my thoughts are not your thoughts, neither are your ways my ways, declares the Lord" (Isaiah 55:8, NIV).

We were tasked with one final permanent change of station and prepared to move back to San Antonio, Texas. I resisted the move for as long as I could, deciding I wanted to continue to live in blissful isolation on the island. It was comfortable, and I wanted to remain in what was comfortable. It would take me a while longer to learn that sometimes God will push you from what's comfortable in order to get the glory from your life!

There was no logical way for me to remain where I was, so I conceded. I began to accept the move, or so I thought, with one caveat. I wanted life as it was before. Before all hell broke loose, but nothing about this move would go as expected.

It wasn't until after my husband retired and accepted a civilian job overseas that I realized God and I were still barely speaking. I started working with a friend who owned a T-shirt shop and worked ten to twelve hours a day, seven days a week. Even on the occasional Sundays off, I wasn't going to church. It took a while longer and a few conversations with a counselor for me to realize I was still depressed. I also realized I was still a little bitter and a lot angry at God. I still hadn't healed, but I was finally ready!

It had been years of feeling forsaken and forgotten, as if God didn't hear my heart crying out from despair. Out of sheer fatigue and desperation, I started clawing my way from the pit I was feeling so comfortable in. I fought to trust God again, reminding myself that God loves me. I tried to stand on the promise that He would never leave me or forsake me, telling myself night and day that I could trust God and the plan He had for my life. It didn't happen overnight. But pretty soon I was able to forgive, conceding that God knew best for me, according to Jeremiah 29:11. It would take a while longer before I was able to forgive myself.

I constantly went back to Isaiah 61:7 (NIV), the end of which says, "...And so you will inherit a double portion in your land, and everlasting joy will be yours." It wasn't long before I could smile and finally mean it.

As I mentioned before, the move to Texas didn't initially go as I had hoped. For starters, we didn't live where we thought we would. As it happened, that particular area had deteriorated and we were advised to move into the next town where we found a beautiful home in a quiet, beautifully landscaped neighborhood. I also didn't attend the same church that I thought I would; my expectations had evolved and I was unable to reconnect with the current membership. However, I began to attend an eChurch, Mountaintop Faith Ministries, online via their livestream. I didn't find a job right away as I anticipated, but worked at completing my bachelor's degree, uninterrupted. I started a blog, wrote books, and learned more about publishing. I was also able to help a family member moving to the area transition to their new home.

I developed a new relationship with God, based on trust and understanding. He was with me through every step of the pain and darkness. I'm thankful most of all that God kept my mind, heart, and spirit. Even as my friends and family were having babies around me, I didn't become bitter or envious; I celebrated with them ... and spoiled their children just a little. I continue to rest in the knowledge that God knows the plans He has for me and I trust His plans are always better than mine.

"...and be content with what you have, because God has said, 'Never will I leave you; never will I forsake you'" (Hebrews13:5, NIV).

I won't lie to you, today, I still don't know why God allowed me to endure the pain of miscarriage. The best I can guess is so I can encourage other women going through the same trial. What I know for sure is that there is life after miscarriage and peace after the storm. And in the midst of your storm, God remembers your hopes, dreams, and most intimate desires. Trust God and His perfect timing. My sister, hold on because you are not forgotten!

About the Author

Cassietta Jefferson is a contemporary Christian author, book reviewer, and blogger. She is the founder of Virtuous Ink Publishing where she seeks to provide her readers with the best in contemporary Christian literature. She earned her Bachelors of Applied Science in Healthcare Administration from Wayland Baptist University.

Cassietta currently resides in Las Vegas Nevada where she lives with her husband of twenty years, retired United States Air Force Master Sergeant Ben Jefferson Jr.

God Sees What We Cannot See

~~~

Angie Jones

The Beginning

I woke up one summer morning thanking God for another day and for watching over and being with me. It was an important day because within a few hours I would be heading to the hospital to have a hysterectomy. The continual problems from having a fibroid tumor, the low energy level, and the many procedures throughout the years are what led me to decide I no longer wanted to deal with those problems again.

As I sat before the Lord, I asked what He would like me to read in the Bible. I felt pressed upon to read

Psalm 91:9-12 (NASB). "For you have made the Lord, my refuge, Even the Most High, your dwelling place. No evil will befall you, Nor will any plague come near your tent. For He will give His angels charge concerning you, To guard you in all your ways. They will bear you up in their hands, That you do not strike your foot against a stone."

These Bible verses brought comfort and questions at the same time. I was comforted knowing that God was with me and He had set His angels charge over me but wondered what was meant by a plague not coming near me. I asked the Lord, "Is there something further I need to pray through regarding this surgery?" As I lay there and pondered, I had peace that He was in control and all would go well with the surgery.

I sensed God's presence as I left for the hospital and throughout the day. The surgery went well and I was able to come home several hours after. As I recovered at home throughout the week, I could not help but think of the new freedom I had embarked upon. No longer would I have to be concerned with the low energy level and having any more procedures. As I entered my second week after the surgery, I could tell things were looking up and I was coming back slowly, but surely, to my old-new self again. I felt like things were progressing well and I was moving around a lot more swiftly. I had made arrangements to work from home while I slowly recovered.

I woke up feeling better than the day before. Every

day was a progression. I was regaining my strength, the pain was subsiding, and I was moving around more swiftly.

Suddenly around mid-morning nine days after surgery, I began to feel extremely fatigued and feverish. I decided to take a break from work and lie down to see if I might begin to feel better. But an hour had gone by and I was not feeling any better, and I still had a low-grade fever. I had to clock out from work for the day. I knew something was not right. Concerned that something could be terribly wrong, I called the doctor's office for advice and to see if that was a normal part of the healing process. After a series of questions, the nurse suggested I go to the emergency room.

The Unveiling

I called all the people I knew could possibly be at home during that time of the day to find they were all out of town or not available to take me to the hospital. I questioned if I really needed to go to the emergency room, but after lying there for over an hour not feeling any better, I had a real sense (a nudging from the Holy Spirit) I needed to go. I had resolved I should not be feeling so terrible, considering just a few hours earlier I was feeling well.

I gathered my things and shuffled my way to the car and drove to the hospital. As I parked the car, I looked for the closest parking spot to the door. I dragged my feet to the entrance that seemed miles away. I finally made it inside and was surprisingly greeted by a prayer team member from my church. In that moment, I really needed to see a familiar face. As soon as I saw her, I cried out, "Something is wrong with me." She quickly and graciously grabbed the nearest wheelchair for me. In pain, I plopped into the seat, and she wheeled me to the counter. I was asked several questions, mostly to determine my level of urgency and whether I was considered a *real* emergency.

A Friday night, it seemed the room was filling quickly. I sat there for a few hours and listened to worship music with my earbud in one ear and anticipated hearing my name being called with the other ear. I really was not feeling any better, so listening to worship music helped me to stay rested, and I could sense God's presence there. After some time, a friend who was visiting her mom at the hospital came to see me while I was in the waiting room, and we talked and prayed together. Time was moving along and the next thing I realized, I had been sitting there for six hours without being seen. I said, "Lord, I do not know why I am still here, but if I need to be here, please help me to stay." A supernatural peace came over me and the time flew by without me even knowing how long I had really been sitting there. The thought came to me, *If I have an infection of some sort from the surgery, I need to know.* It was that thought that kept me in the emergency room. By the eighth hour of sitting there, I finally had enough energy to get up to find out what was going on. The attendant stated the computers had gone down and they had stopped taking patients for over three hours, and I was next in line. If I were not next, I would have decided to go home. Another friend came to the ER to sit with me, and within a half an hour, I was being seen. By then, I was feeling better, but still very exhausted.

As I was wheeled into the room, I had a sense of relief that I was finally going to find out what was going on with me. The doctor came to the room and asked some questions, then decided to check for a bladder infection. And, if that came back negative, they would do a CT scan. The bladder infection test was negative.

When the results came back from the CT scan, the doctor calmly walked into the room and said, "You do not have any infections from the surgery, but you do have masses on your pancreas and liver that need to get checked out as soon as possible."

"Is it cancer?" I asked.

He said, "I cannot tell you what the masses are. You will have to make an appointment, and I have made the referral to the gastrointestinal (GI) department."

In the meantime, the emergency room doctor had called the on-call OB/GYN doctor. When she came in, I was still a little preoccupied with the news of having masses on my pancreas and liver. She said, "I know you! I was in the operating room during your surgery, so I can attest that your surgery went well. You just need to rest and let your body recover, and you need to look further into the masses on your pancreas and liver. How you are feeling has to do with you not resting well."

My friend and I hugged and walked to our cars. I got into the car and looked at the clock and realized I had been in the emergency room for over twelve hours. As I sat in the car for a minute, I was relieved there were no complications from the surgery. But at the same time I was concerned about the masses on my pancreas and liver. Then a quick thought came to my mind. This emergency room visit was not about complications with the surgery, it was about the masses that needed to be revealed.

God Was Silent

Seeing that it was after midnight by the time I left the emergency room, I was exhausted and just wanted to sleep. I really didn't think too much about all that had just happened. When I woke up the following morning, after googling "masses on pancreas and liver," I began to seriously ponder the thought I might have cancer. There was nothing in the Google search results to indicate I didn't have cancer. In fact, I read that pancreatic cancer is often found when it's too late and has spread to other organs. My mind was going toward the worst case scenario. There was something very real about what was happening to me. I was not talking to someone else about their issue. This was not a dream. Not something I was reading about. This was actually happening to me. I was actually being faced with the fact I just might have cancer. Trying to keep my mind from thinking the worst was a battle since I had not been to the doctor yet. I decided that I wasn't going to talk too much about this to anyone at this point. Because one, I did not have much information and knowledge as to what was really going on. And two, I wanted to hear what God was saying about all this.

As I sat before the Lord that morning, he was silent. He wasn't saying anything. He was watching me. I had a real sense of His presence, and I was sure He was watching how I would respond. Would I fall apart emotionally and allow fear to dominate? What would I be saying regarding what was happening? Would I begin to speak words of life or words of death? How would I react to what could possibly be the worst news of my life?

I had decided when I walked into the gastrointestinal doctor's office that Monday by myself, I would not assume the worst. Well, that was until the doctor said I should prepare for the worst, and based upon his experience, the tumor on my pancreas was most likely cancer. Although he could not say for sure until the biopsy, he gave no indication this could possibly be anything other than cancer. He shared the CT (computerized tomography) scan that showed the 4 cm tumor on my pancreas (which four weeks later measured 4.5 cm) and the 1 cm mass on my liver was fluid-filled and not of concern. While there, he contacted the surgeon who confirmed the grave concern regarding the tumor on my pancreas. Later that day, the surgeon called me and said the tumor needed to be biopsied, but more importantly it needed to come out as soon as possible. He wanted to schedule the surgery as early as the next two weeks. However, I did not feel like I was physically ready for another surgery. It had only been two weeks since the previous one. I knew I needed to recover from my first surgery before the next. I prayed I did not have to have the surgery in two weeks. I needed more time to heal from the hysterectomy.

Once I left the doctor's office, I sat in my car for about fifteen minutes. I really did not want to believe this was happening and began to think, *How am I going to handle this news?* I knew in that moment I did not fully have the answer to that question; I also knew I really did not want to talk much about it.

I became very aware life and death were before me, and I was in a battle for my life. I decided to share the news with my pastors and just a few friends who I knew would pray for me while I processed and made a decision on how I was going to position myself for the battle ahead.

Positions for the Battle: Keys to Victory

The Mind Battle

Often when we are faced with challenging situations, our minds will take over, and we will automatically lean in the direction of the worst case scenario. We mull over and over in our minds all the what ifs: What could we have done differently? Why did this happen to me? What am I going to do now? Our mind is one of the greatest battlefields. We may struggle with physical ailments, situations, and circumstances, but the victory begins in the mind. It does not really matter what goes on in our circumstances, it matters more what we think during our circumstances. What we think reflects in our behavior, and how we will feel emotionally is an indication of what we are thinking. Proverbs 4:23 (NCV) says, "Be careful what you think, because your thoughts run your life." Second Corinthians 10: 5 (NIV) says "We demolish arguments and every pretension that sets itself up against the knowledge of God, and we take captive every thought to make it obedient to Christ."

We have options and they begin with how we think. Our battle is taking our thoughts before the Lord and asking if this is coming from Him or not. If the thought is not coming from Him, then we can reject it and think about and ask the Lord to help with the struggling thoughts. We have to stop ourselves and recognize what we are thinking so we can bring that thought to the Lord. Uncontrolled thoughts equal an uncontrolled life.

I knew that capturing my thoughts during this difficult time would be extremely important to my victory. I knew if I allowed myself to continually go to the worst case scenario, I would somehow end up in the very place of that thought. As I was processing through my thoughts, I determined in my mind that God was the one who had started this process by revealing the growing tumor. Therefore, He was going to finish it by healing me completely. Because I had no significant symptoms, I had no idea there was a large tumor growing on my pancreas. I did not feel sick and would occasionally have a dull pain that I recognized after I learned of the tumor. It became clear to me that God saw the tumor and wanted to do something about it, hence the real reason for going to the emergency room that day. It was that very thought that God wanted me healed that kept me moving toward healing in every thought. I might not like the process of my healing by having the surgery and possibly chemotherapy, but in the end, I knew I would be healed. I knew that God would finish His work. I knew that my life was not over and decided this was what I would say to people when I talked about my ordeal. God saw it and wanted to do something about it.

Every time I started to feel sad, scared, or especially anxious, I had to catch myself and think about *what* I was thinking about. Think about what you are thinking about, especially when you are feeling any negative feelings. How you feel has a lot to do with what you are thinking about. Our thought life is very powerful and leads our life. Our minds can create scenarios that can bless us or hinder us from receiving the promises of God.

Get Promises from the Bible

There are many opportunities where thought adjustments have to be made during tough situations. Thought adjustments are simply where we continually align our thoughts with the promises and the Word of God. What promise has God given you? What scripture can you stand upon during your difficult time? All the promises of God are Yes and Amen. God says what He means and means what He says. There are no words on this Earth greater than the words of God. It is up to us to fill our minds with His words and promises and to feed our faith. There are many different ways we can do this: read the Bible, download an app on your phone where you can listen to several different versions of the Bible, listen to various podcasts, YouTube videos with inspirational messages and songs from strong Christian leaders and worshippers. There are so many different ways to feed your faith, we are without excuse.

On the day of my first surgery, I did not know how important the scripture the Lord gave me that morning would become. It was one of the scriptures I stood on during that difficult time. I kept myself in remembrance of the fact "No plague would come near me." Though I didn't understand it at the time the Lord gave it to me, it became clearer to me nine days later as I sat in the doctor's office, and he told me to prepare for the worst.

In the weeks to follow, I looked up many scriptures on healing and posted them where I could read them throughout the days before my surgery. The Bible is full of promises that you can completely rely upon. There are no greater words on this earth than His Word. The Bible is the ultimate source for healing, comfort, deliverance, peace, direction, and—any and everything—we could possibly need in this lifetime. His Word is the only word that is living; it is alive and active and powerful enough to change a situation and a life. Words alone do not heal, but it is the Spirit of God that gives life to the words. The words that are filled with God's life will heal, change, and deliver. We can speak many words, but it is the power of God that gives life, healing, and deliverance as we speak and agree with His words.

It was during a prayer time with my (at the time) eleven-year-old son who had been diagnosed with *ADHD* since six, that I was reading and praying scripture after scripture on healing over him that God completely healed him. Before the healing, I would get calls from his teachers and principal on a regular basis because he was continually disruptive in class. He had to continually be monitored and without medication he was completely out of control. So the day I ran out of medication, I was desperate and called him into the room and said, "Let's pray." I began to pray healing scripture after healing scripture over him, and the power of God's Word healed him. "For the Word of God is alive and powerful. It is sharper than the sharpest two-edged sword, cutting between soul and spirit, between joint and marrow. It exposes our innermost thoughts and desires. Nothing in all creation is hidden from God" (Hebrews 4:12, NLT).

Remember what God has spoken to you in the past. When you write down and keep track of the past words the Lord has spoken, you will have a track record of His faithfulness. And when the hard times come and when God is silent, you will have a record of the words and scriptures He has spoken to you in the past to stand on. God's silence is not an indication that He is not there because the Word says in Psalm 46:1(NASB), "God is our refuge and strength, a very present help in trouble," and Deuteronomy 31:6 (NASB) says, "Be strong and courageous, do not be afraid or tremble at them, for the Lord your God is the one who goes with you. He will not fail you or forsake you."

He is there in our times of trouble. Sometimes we have to speak what we already know to be truth. We have to remind ourselves and God of the things He has spoken and pay attention to the small things that let us know God is present.

Worship

Worship is a fast way to make a quick mind adjustment. When you worship God, you are no longer thinking about all the what ifs, but the One who is the All-Sufficient One. He is our Healer, Peace-Giver, Provider, and the creator of the universe. There is no one to compare Him to.

Worship shifts our mindsets. It changes us from the inside out. Worshipping God delivers us from ourselves and from the enemy. Our focus becomes God. He is worthy to be praised in the good times and in the bad times. The enemy hates when we worship God because he wants to be worshipped. When we turn our worship toward God, the devil does not like that and cannot stay in the presence of anyone who is worshipping God. When our focus becomes God-alone in our worship, there is no room for the enemy.

Worship is a key that brings forth healing. There

were many days I had to worship through the feelings of not wanting to go through this ordeal. There was a fight within myself to feel sorry for myself, but worship kept those feelings from taking precedence. I would sing songs that had words like, "No weapon formed against me shall prosper ..." and "You alone deserve the glory. You alone deserve the praise. By your blood you have redeemed us, washed away all guilt and shame. I will praise you in the morning ..." Worship put my mind at ease and made room for God to work in my heart and life.

Find Your Village

A village represents a small community of people who will support and watch out for one another in one way or another. God never meant for us to live this life alone and separated from others. We need other people in our lives. We need the body of Christ. We need people we can call on in our time of need. Family is wonderful and will be there for you, but sometimes people do not have supportive family members and the church family becomes their family. Being connected to a local church gives us an extended family and extended support. My family and extended family played such an important role in my recovery during both my surgeries by bringing me food, going to the store, sitting in the hospital, coming to stay with me during my critical time after my surgeries, sending me encouraging words, picking up my kids for me, and checking on me. If I had no support at all, I am sure my recovery would have taken longer. We need one another.

Trust God

Trust requires a letting go. Knowing who you are letting go *to* makes the difference in whether or not you can trust them. God has a track record that we can count on. He is a man of His Word; He never will leave or forsake us. He has proven to be All-Powerful. He has proven He is able to do creative miracles. He has proven that He is the All-Sufficient One, and that He knows all things. God sees what we cannot see and He is working for our good. He is the creator of the universe, heaven and earth, and He is our creator. He knows everything about our bodies and our life.

Trust is like jumping out of an airplane with a parachute. Once you jump, you cannot decide in the middle of going down you do not want to do this. You have to rely upon your well-maintained, well-equipped parachute to bring you to the ground safely. Trust in God comes easier when you are connecting with Him on a regular basis in one way or another, learning His track record, and faithfulness and love toward you. Fear hinders trust. When it is time to fully rely upon God, we are able to with confidence because we know in whom we are relying upon to get us through.

THE VICTORY

First, it is a miracle that I stayed in the emergency room for eight hours before even being seen. It was only by His grace and Him overshadowing me that I remained in such an uncomfortable place for so long. He was determined to protect me from the plans of the enemy. The devil has no power over our lives. God is truly working all things for our good.

The healing began as I prayed with different people. Throughout the time before the surgery, there were specific prayers that were prayed that every cancer cell would die. I believe God saw every cancer cell and I knew—with no doubt—that God was answering those specific prayers. I knew it was the combination of the removal of the tumor and the prayers of many people that I was healed completely. God completely annihilated the plans of the enemy.

After the surgery, I received my biopsy report that said the tumor was benign. Praise God! That is a miracle in itself. After reading the report, four doctors confirmed God's faithfulness. First, the surgeon said the tumor was removed just in time because it probably would have been cancerous. I was grateful to hear that. Second, my mom (step-mom) sent my biopsy report to my sister-in-law, a nurse practitioner, who in turn had her presiding doctor look at the report and report the tumor was removed just in time. Third, the oncologist said the tumor was large enough and at a stage where cancer would have probably been inevitable had it remained; he confirmed there was no need for chemotherapy. Hallelujah! Lastly, my primary physician stated that it was good the tumor was removed because there was a high possibility it would not have ended well. Four *different* doctors confirming the Greatness of God! God sees what we do not see and He is working it out for our good. We may not see and understand everything—but He does.

About the Author

Angie Jones is passionate about prayer and called to build prayer within the local church. Since the late 1980s, she has been involved with prayer ministries through intercessory prayer as a watchman on the wall, corporate prayer, prayer walks, prayer partners, and facilitating prayer meetings and conferences. She wrote a monthly publication "The Prayer Journal" which included articles on prayer, testimonies and prayer activities. As a co-leader of Community Prayer Conference Call connecting local churches in prayer, she leads a team of eighty-plus prayer team members and holds prayer trainings within the local church.

An advocate for adoption, Angie lives in Fairfield, CA and is the mother of three adopted children.

Hope Exists

Sydney DeLa Torre

When I was forty-one, my life completely spun out of control. Everything I'd worked the last fifteen years of my life to achieve would be dissolved over the next fifteen months. While I can share the details of the events that collectively led to *my fall* from grace, I had to discover the root issue that contributed to the mess my life had become. I lacked peace and longed for the relief that can only come through God. The only one who could offer clarity and help.

Before this chapter of my life began, the stage was being set. Looking back at the events of my life, it may have been understandable to attach my poor choices and sin to the neglect I lived through as a toddler; the severe emotional, physical, and sexual abuses I suffered as a child; the long-reaching damage I experienced from growing up in an alcoholic home; abusive boyfriends who used and disrespected me; the struggles of being a single teen mom; and the devastation of losing my mom to cancer when I was twenty-two.

But that line of thinking only allows justification to enter in. The truth is: I had less than a perfect upbringing and have dealt with more than my share of trauma.

This is just a chapter of my life story. An account of how pain hardened my heart against my heavenly Father and the destructive path I chose before returning home to Him. A testimony of how God prevailed through the bleakness of my life to show me that hope can exist when you place it in Him. A praise as I share how God enabled me to arise from the ashes of my life and renewed me through His love, mercy and grace. I open the pages of my story to you, not to glorify anything that I did, but rather to testify to the transformational love and grace that Jesus Christ offered me. The same love and grace that's available to you.

⚭

It was a beautiful spring day. The cherry blossoms were in full bloom and the sun was shining for all to see. The sun perched high in the sky sent warm beams through our window to wrap me in comfort as I sat crying on our couch. I cried out to God, "Please help me. I don't know how to move forward. I feel so alone. How could this happen, God? We moved here to be a light in this community and now all I see is darkness. I agreed I would do whatever it takes to serve you, but I never expected my kids to get hurt. *How could YOU allow this to happen?!*"

Before long I would find myself standing in our family room, literally yelling at God. Yelling, because I was hurt and disappointed. Yelling, because I was afraid. Yelling, because in that moment I refused to be comforted. I wanted to be angry. In fact, I was outraged. Yelling, because I lived my life believing bad things would happen to me because deep inside I felt unworthy. Yelling, because God (and I) were supposed to protect my children from the same pain that I experienced as a child. Yelling, because my life was out of control ... *my control* ... Had I ever really surrendered it to God? Or did I attempt to surrender it, only to pick it back up and fail to lay it down again?

This would prove to be a pivotal moment. A moment that changed the course of my life. As I stood there yelling at God, I never stopped to listen. I never asked for forgiveness for the way I expressed the anger and wrath I was feeling. I didn't read my Bible. I didn't ask Him to take the pain away and help me heal. In that moment, instead of giving my burdens to the Lord, in my heart, I held God responsible for what had happened to us.

Early Easter morning, as I was helping my youngest son (who is cognitively delayed) get ready for church, he shared heartbreaking news. He revealed he had been molested. My heart sank. The next several months would involve Child Protective Services investigations, meetings, counseling, and court. We did our best to navigate these events. My husband and I chose to forgive the people who transgressed against us. My husband would hold himself responsible for moving our family near this *sexual predator*. I would hold myself responsible for failing to protect my son and for trusting a friend to babysit him. We both were traumatized and felt we had failed as parents. We didn't stop long enough to experience the healing God could have provided us. We neglected the promise of Psalm 55:22, (NLT): "Give your burdens to the Lord, and He will take care of you. He will not permit the godly to slip and fall."

The truth is, I have always internalized all the pain and confusion I felt. I deceived myself by thinking I was healing from this. The pain of life's disappointments, rejection and feelings of betrayal all lay festering under the veneer of my need for everything to be okay. I had made myself so busy with helping others and overcommitting to projects that I had no time to pray or read the Bible. We stopped going to church. We stopped praying. The pain was so great we avoided talking about it and stopped talking to each other. We stopped talking to God. Over the next few months, everything that was buried within my emotional holding tank would churn and swirl.

Before too long, we found ourselves welcoming my sister into our home. She needed a place to stay after being released from a drug and alcohol rehabilitation program. Prior to coming to stay with us, my sister invited a man she met during rehab to our home without letting us know. My husband worked away from home during the week and returned on the weekends. This would afford my sister the chance to have her friend come over during the week for dinner or a movie. The problem was *he* didn't want to leave. He stayed. This man embodied everything I detested. He was loud, arrogant, disrespectful, misogynistic, abusive, and vile. My sister disregarded my many requests to get him to leave.

One night I asked him to leave my home. He refused. My sister pleaded to let him stay. I gave in to her request as I didn't know how to get this unwanted guest to leave and I didn't want to fight with her. The next morning, as I was getting ready to leave for work, my husband called. Thinking I was alone in my home, I shared my fears and concerns. He assured me he would return home that evening to deal with this man. Overhearing the fears I'd shared with my husband, this unwanted guest would use brute force and become verbally abusive to challenge and confront me. He would utterly terrorize and traumatize me before leaving for good. I would compose myself before shoving these new feelings down. I wouldn't share with anyone how degraded and afraid this man made me feel. It would be one more thing I would hide away from myself and God.

God warns us in Jeremiah 17:9 (NLT): "The human heart is the most deceitful of all things, and desperately wicked. Who really knows how bad it is?" My heart *was* desperately wicked and deceitful. It deceived me and turned away from God. During this time, our best friends had picked up on the seriousness of my mental state and suggested my family be proactive. This translated to my family having me arrested on a 5150 (danger to yourself or others). Admitting me to a psychiatric hospital was probably God's way of helping me deal with my pain and dissect all those overwhelming feelings. The problem was I refused God's help and got even angrier. I was hurt—*yet* again.

I had suffered an emotional breakdown and needed professional help. The invisible tank that held all my pain, hurt, disappointments, and irrational fears had burst wide open. Crushing emotions that had been festering months to decades spewed out like lava from a volcano. All I needed to do was let go, surrender, and trust God for my healing. My heart was hardened. I chose to fight, but not against the enemy of my soul. I chose to fight my husband, family, and doctors. The fury of endless emotions and illogical thoughts clouded my ability to make rational decisions.

Now I had to convince these people that although I was an emotional wreck, I wasn't suicidal. Which meant I would lie. Before my family admitted me, I *had* purposed to end it all. I certainly needed help, but I was blindsided by their approach. Confused, I felt betrayed by my family. I was hurt by their actions. I felt unloved. All my thoughts were infiltrated with the painful, angry hurts and resentments that had been buried for years, now loosed to stain my mind's eye. As calmly as I could, I rehearsed the details of my imaginary story.

Amid all this pain and confusion, I erected a wall of fear and resentment. I tapped into a coil of rebellion that had been restrained inside my flesh until now, waiting to break free. Who could I trust? I refused to receive the way out God had made for me. Dark thoughts and feelings relentlessly pounded away on my being until the enemy burst the door open to my will and intellect and was working overtime to divide, devour, and kill. Many voices were going through my mind. All of which had the power to influence my next step: either to get help and surrender to God, or run away from help, turn my back on God, and make an even bigger mess of my life. If only I had hit my knees and cried out to God.

Somehow, I managed to convince those people I was well enough to be released. The problem was, I unknowingly chose to turn towards a path that would lead me to the biggest moral failures of my life. Up until then, the pain I was feeling had been inflicted from outside myself. Sick in the mind and tormented, my life journey would be saturated with the self-inflicted pain of my desperately destructive choices and lies. It would seem the enemy was successful in dividing our family—and so was I.

In order to get released, someone other than my husband needed to pick me up and take responsibility for me. My mind raced ... who could I call? I called a family friend who was close enough to our family to know the tragedies we were experiencing.

The first thing he said after picking me up was, "How could your husband have done this to you? I would never have locked you up."

I could feel anger bubbling up inside. I felt shame and humiliation!

As I attempted to go back to work in the following days, I would find I'd lost the ability to do my job. I lost the ability to function at all. Pain and anger consumed every part of my being. My nervous system continued revolting with thick, itchy red hives all over my face and body, non-stop heart palpitations, substantial weight loss, horrific stomach pain, unpredictable bouts of crying, and falling asleep without warning during the day. All this unresolved trauma led me into a clinical depression. The person I used to be, was hopelessly lost to me.

Shortly after returning to work, I fell asleep while driving the eighteen miles between my daughter's school and my job. Somehow, I miraculously made it to her campus where I promptly fell asleep in my car. I awoke to a pounding on my window. One of my daughter's friends was peering down at me with a huge smile on her face.

"What are you doing?" She beamed.

I wiped the sleep from my eyes and opened the door. "I fell asleep driving here and I don't know how I'm going to make it home. I need something to help me wake up."

She casually said, "I can get anything you want."

I hadn't been referring to drugs, yet I knew that's *exactly* what she meant. The person I was before the breakdown would *never* have entertained this conversation. I hadn't done drugs or alcohol of any type since I gave my heart to Jesus at twenty-six years old.

My daughter's classmate dumped her purse out on the front seat of her car. Frantically searching through its contents, she grabbed what looked like a piece of rock salt. She smiled and instructed, "Take this, crush it, and snort it. I promise it will do the trick."

I didn't ask what it was; I only asked if it was addictive and was told it wasn't.

As soon as I had my daughter in the car, we drove across the street to Starbucks. I ran into the bathroom, crushed the rock and snorted it. As I was walking out of the restroom, a feeling of euphoria hit me like nothing I had ever experienced before. I didn't feel *wired*, but rather for the first time in almost a year, I *felt* good! I *felt* more than good, I *felt* everything was going to be okay! I *felt* happy to be alive! Nothing had changed about my circumstances. I'd altered my mind with what turned out to be crystal meth.

As for being addictive ... crystal meth imprints the brain and a person gets addicted within the first five uses. I got addicted with the first use and would continue using this drug to help me *cope*.

As I self-medicated with crystal meth, any shadow of my former self would evaporate. My moral compass would become non-existent. My addiction would consume me and I lied to cover it up. I left my job on disability. I moved to a *bad* part of town to befriend my new-found drug-addicted friends. Everything I previously warned my children never to do, I would go on to do. The war waged against my husband and family—through my actions—was wounding and brutal. The enemy had been given a foothold, and he wasn't going to stop until our family was destroyed.

Hebrews 13:5 (NKJV): "I will never leave you nor forsake you." I was too numb to realize that deep inside I was mad at God. I would talk to Him while I was high or lonely, but I never talked to Him about all the events that brought me to this place. God wasn't done with me either. Once, I mustered up enough courage and walked into a random church and sat in the back. After service I went up and asked for prayer.

The pastor asked, "Anything specific?"

I said, "Just whatever you're led to pray."

The pastor concluded with, "Prodigal, it's time to go home."

I started crying and left.

Just to make sure I didn't think that was a coincidence, a few weeks later, God used an ultrasound technician to speak to me.

The ultrasound tech told me, "I'm not supposed to do this ... I could get in trouble ... but I feel so impressed I'm supposed to pray for you..." She paused, "Did you hear me? Is it okay if I pray for you?"

Now, mind you, up to this point the only thing I had said to this lady was, "Where do I sit?"

I responded, "If you feel you must."

She began praying and finished her prayer by saying, "God wants you to know everything is going to be okay. He loves you. He's going to heal you. God wants *you*, His prodigal, to come home."

Hot tears streamed down my face. My voice quivered, "Thank you. Now could you please stop?!" And she did, but not before admitting she had never prayed for a patient before.

Eventually, my family would expose my lies and confront my drug addiction. They offered to help, but I didn't trust them anymore. I would be evicted from my apartment and check into a hotel. That night I called family, asking for help. They were exhausted by my lies, manipulation, and tactics, and refused to help. No one would help me.

After I checked out the next morning, I stood looking at all my worldly possessions shoved in my car. I got in the car and sat there. I had no money, no gas, no food, no drugs, no friends, and no family. I had a razor and pulled it out of my wallet. I held it to my wrist and cried out to God ... "No one loves me anymore ... No one cares ... Please, God, let me die. Help me. It hurts so bad." I started to press the sharp blade against my bony wrist. I was startled by a woman pounding on my window screaming, "Don't do it. I call police. It's okay." The maid had been watching me as I sat in my car. She wanted to help me, but all I heard was, "I call police."

I started my car and fled as fast as I could. I convinced a stranger to help me with a half a tank of gas. I drove around with nowhere to go until I pulled over and fell asleep. It was dark when I woke up. I called out to God for help. The words of the pastor and the ultrasound tech came to my mind. "Prodigal, go home." I started my car and headed towards home.

Home. A place I hadn't been in almost a year. I was surprised the front door was unlocked when I arrived. I walked in to find a couple of church interns were now residing in our home. They greeted me and inquired if I was allowed to be there. I hastily retorted, "It's my home. Why wouldn't I be allowed to be here?" They promptly disappeared. Within ten minutes, my husband showed up, told me to leave, then called the police.

I refused to leave until I got to see my youngest son. Just then his school bus pulled up. As he exited the bus, I was overwhelmed with emotions. He had grown so much; he was so big. My heart ached so bad in that moment. I wanted to hug him. I realized I had no business being there. How selfish had I been? While I was feeling sorry for myself, allowing my emotions to overtake me, I'd abandoned my family. They, too, were drowning in their own trauma and pain.

I thought about leaving until I saw my son's expression as he recognized me. His face lit up; he smiled a huge smile. He walked over and threw his arms around me. As the warmth and weight of my baby boy's strong arms wrapped around my diminished ninety-five-pound frame, he kissed my cheek and said, "I love you, Mom. I miss you. Are you going to come home now?" *He told me he loved me.* I needed to hear that. God was using my son to tangibly love me. Just an hour before, I was crying out to God, "No one loves me or wants me ... Please give me a reason to live."

I told my son I wanted to stay, but Dad wanted me to leave. The police came and informed my husband he couldn't kick me out, as I had a legal right to be there. I stayed.

The next three months consisted of God breaking down the walls that were erected over the previous year. Initially, no one in the house would acknowledge or even talk to me. I slept in my son's room on the floor. God would continue working behind the scenes to reunite our family, despite ourselves. I was finally home, but it had become just a house. All the joy and love that we once shared as a family was gone. I kept getting high and lying.

Eventually, my husband and I went out of town and visited a friend's church. That night the pastor stepped over to my husband in the middle of the service to ask if I was his wife. The pastor asked him five times before I revealed I was his wife.

He told my husband, "I don't know you or your family or why you came here tonight. I believe God wants me to tell you something. I'm supposed to tell you everything is going to be okay. I don't know your story, but the Lord wants you to know even though you don't trust her now, He is going to restore her, so you can trust her again."

My husband cried and shook his head *no*.

The pastor continued, "God wants you to know you can trust Him for *her*."

God dared my husband to hope again, and gave him the longing of his heart, to have his family made whole, beginning with me. Proverbs 13:12, (NIV) tells us, "Hope deferred makes the heart sick: but a longing fulfilled is a tree of life."

I wanted my life to change from what I had made it to the beautiful masterpiece God intended it to be. I wanted restoration, forgiveness, peace, and joy. I knew God was demanding total surrender. This meant I would offer to check into an inpatient rehabilitation program. It also meant I would have to acknowledge all the horrific lies I'd told, take responsibility for my actions, seek forgiveness, forgive others, and make amends. There was no way I would be able to do this on my own. Total surrender and faith in the one who knew me better than I knew myself was what it would take for me to get a new life. God declares, "For I know the plans I have for you," declares the Lord, "plans to prosper you and not to harm you, plans to give you hope and a future" (Jeremiah 29:11, NIV).

When the extreme events of my life started crashing over me, like waves in a torrential sea, I lost hope. *Hope* in Scripture means *a strong and confident expectation.* **As I trusted and surrendered to God, He made me whole. He gave me His strength, comfort, and grace. He enabled me to confront my demons and forgive myself.** As I continued to surrender all to God, He restored my marriage. He restored my health. He renewed my mind. He renewed my spirit.

God wants you to know that hope exists through His son Jesus. No matter what crisis you may find yourself facing, God will make a way where there seems to be no way. "Cast all your anxiety on him because he cares for you" (1 Peter 5:7, NIV). It's never too late to turn back to our heavenly Father. He's waiting—arms open wide—for us to completely surrender ourselves to Him.

You'll know you're surrendered when you rely on God to work things out, instead of manipulating or forcing your agenda to try to control the situation.

Surrendering to God and trusting Him with my pain allowed me to completely heal and achieve and maintain sobriety. Today, I have achieved eleven years drug-free. My husband and I just celebrated our twenty-seventh year of marriage. God allowed me to arise from the ashes of my life and redeemed my past to help start a Christian recovery group. I am always blessed, when given a chance to share my testimony, how many people comment they would never have known I was an addict. That's the power of Jesus Christ. "Therefore, if anyone is in Christ, the new creation has come. The old has gone, the new is here" (2 Corinthians 5:17, NIV)

About the Author

Sydney DeLa Torre is creative, passionate and funny. She has a heart for God that exudes in her writing. Her transparency and vulnerability are on display as she walks her audience through the fragments of her broken life so God may be glorified. Sydney has always been encouraged by others to "share her story." From after school children's programs to women and youth groups, her words open the window to her heart. Often witty, Sydney approaches some of life's toughest challenges with candor, honesty and an understanding that no problem is too big for God.

Personal discoveries, as well as spiritual growth, have proven to be a source of inspiration for her writings. Her works introduce real flawed characters who overcome obstacles through Jesus. Currently penning her first fiction novel, about God's love and grace breaking down barriers and transforming hearts, she hopes to complete it soon.

Sydney and her husband, William, reside in the breathtaking mountains of Arnold, California.

Back Down Memory Lane

Michele Mills

"For I know the thoughts that I think toward you, saith the Lord, thoughts of peace, and not of evil, to give you an expected end" (Jeremiah 29:11, KJV).

I never thought, in my wildest dreams, I would ever experience my much-loved mother, Lillie Mae Christopher, having to deal with the unpredictable and dreadful diseases: *Dementia, Congestive Heart Failure, and COPD.*

Let us take a stroll back down memory lane. Northern California. One day while relaxing in my comfortable recliner. I began to reflect on the years when my mother was first diagnosed with Congestive Heart Failure and COPD.

My mother worked faithfully at the United States Postal Service, retiring after twenty-five years of dedicated service. She used to be a *sharp cookie,* especially when it came to spelling tough words. She welcomed the challenge. She was also an excellent tax preparer for many of our family members and friends.

Growing up I can recall my mother being an avid smoker. She was accustomed to smoking cigarettes since her early high school days. Numerous attempts were made trying to kick the habit, and she was successful for about a year. However, the stresses of life and its variables, had a way of drawing her right back to what some called *cancer sticks.*

I can bring to mind some of my mother's delicious home-cooked meals. She was an incredible cook and was known for her specialty dishes: string beans with cut-up red potatoes; her incredible meatloaf and cabbage; her world-famous salmon croquets with smothered potatoes; the best potato salad ever; her award-winning banana pudding, and a host of other dishes.

My mother was especially gifted with her hands. Her creativity never ceased to amaze me. Once she made a beautiful, fitted, white, long evening dress for her niece to wear to the Junior Prom. She also made her niece a dazzling red dress that she wore and was selected Homecoming Queen.

My mother and her cousin did various creative

projects together. They refurbished the furniture in our home; it was amazing to see the finished product. I recollect for my wedding they made a beautiful, array of blue floral arrangements to decorate the church. The flowers and carnation bouquets for the bridesmaids, the boutonnières for the groomsmen, and the centerpieces for each table at the reception hall were all beautifully handcrafted with their special touch. The floral designs of love and handmade creativity made me feel very special on that day. I was so grateful and told them they should start a business.

I have fond memories of her seventy-fifth birthday celebration. The family and I planned a birthday dinner at HS Lordships in Berkeley. I washed, colored, pressed, and curled my mother's hair. Then we went to the nail salon for a French manicure and spa pedicure. It was her first time visiting a nail salon, simply because my mother always polished her own nails and feet. I dressed her in a nice outfit with matching shoes. Her accessories were matching pearl earrings, necklace, and bracelet. The end result, she looked *fabulous*. And interestingly enough—she knew it. Praise God, the family showered her with beautiful gifts. One of my co-workers made delicious strawberry cupcakes for our celebration. There was so much love in the air, and we took tons of pictures to capture the memorable moments.

My daughter, Adrienne Gaddis, and my mother were very close and shared special times together.

From time to time, Adrienne would drive my mother around town to take care of her errands in my mother's Buick Regal. When my mother was trying to quit smoking, she would sneak on the back porch with Adrienne and they would smoke cigarettes together. When they came back into the house, they did not let on they had been smoking. But I could smell the nicotine and smoke aroma. They had an amazing relationship I always admired.

My mother's parents passed away before she made it to high school. Therefore, I did not get a chance to meet my grandparents and never experienced being a granddaughter. For this reason, I knew when I had grandchildren, I would most certainly follow in my mother's footsteps. Mirroring the closeness and the sacrifices my mother made for my children.

Gradually, she changed her eating habits. She went from home cooked meals to buying cheap TV dinners, pot pies, and many items that were high in sodium content.

My son and I were home with my mother when we noticed both of her ankles were swollen. At the time we thought the swelling was from her daily walks to the nearby gas station to get her lottery tickets. We believed eventually her ankles would return to normal; however, it took longer than we thought. We decided to take her to the doctor for an examination. What we thought would be a regular medical appointment would change our lives. Her admission into the hospital was the beginning of the reoccurring visits to emergency, which were at least three or four times each month.

The doctor had a serious conversation with my mother and discussed the diagnosis of heart disease. He said her lungs were collapsing, and if she did not stop smoking, she could end up using an oxygen tank to breathe, or even die. Incredibly, my mother took this life-threatening news seriously. The doctor's recommendation was an eye opener for her. She immediately lost the desire to inhale another cigarette. It was a miracle.

However, unfortunately my mother's entire world was invaded and altered. She could no longer freely eat her desired foods. The nutritionist placed her on a sodium-restricted diet, and a mild exercise program to strengthen her heart. She was advised to use two inhalers a day.

As time progressed, my mother deviated from the doctor's orders, the nutritionist's program, and even listening to me. Once again, we were back and forth to the hospital emergency room, and each time the doctor would admit her. Every time my mother would forget where the bathroom was located. I knew something was starting to fester in her mind. She would become confused.

I was still in denial. I continued in prayer, crying out to the Lord for my mother to change and listen. I also had to pray for myself because I was getting very frustrated with her behavior, which was not helping the matter. It was such a battle trying to convince my mother to listen and obey the doctor's orders. She was strong-willed and stubborn, set in her ways. We had to resume our many visits, back and forth to Kaiser Hospital. These episodes caused me to miss a great deal of work. God promised me favor with man, so my employers had compassion with my situation and were lenient with me. Thankfully, my mother finally gave in and let me start preparing her meals as the nutritionist had advised.

Let us go further down memory lane. My daughter, Adrienne, was finally able to witness my mother's behavior during the early stages when she took her to Las Vegas to the casinos. They went into the restroom together, but when Adrienne came out of the stall my mother was gone. She had wandered off into the casino.

Adrienne immediately telephoned me, crying. "Momma! I can't find Granny!" So scared, she explained what happened.

I assured her everything was going to be alright. "You will find her, baby."

After we hung up the phone, I began to pray. Thank God Adrienne located my mother standing with a security guard.

Later that night in their hotel room, my mother was really confused. She thought she was at home looking for her bedroom and her house slippers. After those two incidents, Adrienne was very concerned and headed home the next day.

The second time my mother wandered off, she was home with my son, Andre Turner, and my grandson, Chase Benjamin Turner. Early that morning, I received a telephone call from my son. "Momma, Granny is gone!"

I asked what he meant.

He replied, "I got up and the front door was wide open, so I looked outside. Then I noticed that one of Granny's bed covers was on the stairs. I went into Granny's bedroom, and she was not there."

I assured him everything was going to be alright and I was on my way. I called my job and made my way over to my mother's house. While I was driving, I began to pray to God saying, "Lord Jesus, please help us find my mother. Please do not let her be lost in the streets of Oakland, California."

My son and a neighbor were out searching in the community for my mother. Soon after I arrived, a neighbor telephoned and said my mother had been located on High Street. Praise God! She was carrying a brown paper bag in one hand and a bed cover in the other.

When my mother returned, I hugged her so tight I could feel her heart beating. I asked if she was okay. "Momma, why did you go out of the door?"

She explained she had seen her great grandchildren, Charnell and Ronal Hendrix III., go out the front door, and she was going to bring them back. It was obvious she was hallucinating.

I scheduled an emergency appointment for her to visit her physician, Dr. Young. He ran several tests and concluded that my mother was dehydrated. It appeared that she needed to consume more liquids. After this episode, we all sacrificed and moved into the house with my mother. This included myself, my daughter and her two children, and my son and one child. It was a very tight fit; however, it was a familiar place for my mother, and we could keep a better eye on her.

Living with my mother, in her house, allowed me to see her situation from another perspective. I noticed she was starting to forget things quite often. I encouraged her to start going to a local senior center to get more movement and activities. No matter how hard I tried, she would say repeatedly, "I am fine right here reading my newspaper."

On another occasion, I enrolled her in an adult daycare. I felt this would give her the opportunity to interact with other seniors, and hopefully, she could participate in various activities. I thought it was a good plan, but a new battle would begin. Every day I had to persuade her to attend the senior program, but she would constantly say, "I don't belong here, I want to go home." She would display aggressive behavior and become agitated with her words. It hurt me to the core, so I started taking her actions personally. At the time, I did not realize her responses were related to the dementia.

Finally, Dr. Young decided to schedule an appointment for my mother to see a neurologist. I could not tell her where we were going, simply because she would put up a fight. Sometimes she would say, "Why are we going in this building?" I would tell her that Dr. Young asked us to come.

My mother loved her physician, Dr. Young, her doctor for over twenty years. It seemed she was able to make him believe she was fine. She thought so. Based on the examination of her behavior and the information that I shared with him about my mother, it was obvious he was not convinced that she was fine.

This was so frustrating and many times I had to cry out to God for strength: "Lord help me. What is happening to my mother? Why is she treating me this way? Doesn't she realize that I love her dearly and I am doing my best? Lord Jesus, I am only one person."

This experience proved to be very hard for me. I decided to share some of the events I was experiencing with my cousin Emylyn, who used to reside in California; she now resides in Flint, Michigan. She recommended I read a book, *The 36-Hour Day: A Family Guide to Caring for People Who Have Alzheimer's Disease, Related Dementias, and Memory Loss*. Thank God! This book, along with the grace of God, truly helped me stop taking personal my mother's responses and behavior.

So now I had the hard struggle of dealing with certain people, looking in from the outside, and trying to tell me what I should be doing for my mother. It was never enough! Someone always had something to say about the care I was giving my mother, or how I should be caring for her. Besides my Heavenly Father, no one could truly see or understood the pain that I was dealing with concerning my mother's welfare. I had many thoughts of her one day losing her entire memory or even worse if her heart stopped.

Many of the naysayers would say I should consider putting her in a home. That was easier said than done. At least for me it was. Here is a woman who had been there for me, through thick and thin. She had made many sacrifices for the sake of her child and her grandchildren. My goal would be to do the same thing for her.

Deep within my soul, I knew my time with my mother was diminishing. I could not bear the thought of letting her go. I would much rather deal with the insensitive opinions of other people, or the family members' constant talk behind my back. The gossip always seemed to find its way back to me. It made me angry, sad, and emotional. There were times when I would let all my emotions build up, and soon enough, I would explode on my family, releasing everything that was bubbling up inside of me.

Most of my outbursts would generally take place at our family gatherings. I knew this was not healthy. I certainly expected more from certain family members, simply because my mother had been there for them. This used to really bother me. For that reason, I had to repent, cry out to God, and ask for forgiveness. I continued to guard my heart, with diligence, from the issues of life concerning my much-loved family. The scriptures clearly state:

"If we confess our sins, he is faithful and just to forgive us our sins, and to cleanse us from all unrighteousness" (1 John 1:9, KJV).

"Create in me a clean heart, O God, And renew a right and steadfast spirit within me" (Psalm 51:10, AMP).

"Keep your heart with all diligence, For out of it spring the issues of life" (Proverbs 4:23, NKJV).

I continued to cry my heart out to God. I needed Him to keep my heart pure, and to remove all ill feelings from my heart toward others. Eventually, I learned to let it go and stop focusing on the naysayers and family members. I had to turn my full attention back on the Lord Jesus Christ, and continue to display the Fruit of the Spirit (Galatians 5:22-23, NKJV). I am a firm believer in these two statements: "Don't judge me till you walk a mile in my shoes or live a day in my life" and "Don't judge me for the choices I make when you don't know the options I had to choose from."

Let us continue down memory lane. My mother was now totally dependent upon me to dress her, change her pull-ups, and prepare her meals daily. She had lost total interest in her favorite activities, such as reading the newspaper, Rubik's cube, word search, and watching TV, Wheel of Fortune, and Jeopardy. She sat at the kitchen table with a blank stare throughout the day. There were days that I could not hold back the tears, so they would flow down my cheeks.

It was evident I missed my mother's energy. Whenever I was in her presence, I would feel heart-wrenching emotions. My mother always managed to say, "Are you okay?" Strangely enough, she could still sense when her daughter was in pain. It touched my heart every time.

Fast forward on memory lane, I never thought I would ever lose my precious, unforgettable daughter, Adrienne Ni'cole Gaddis, on October 9, 2016. Shockingly, she was twenty-nine years old when she unexpectedly passed away in her sleep. I could not believe the Lord was allowing me to experience such an immense amount of pain and grief—losing my dear daughter. Nor did I ever think I would be the primary caregiver to my much-loved mother, Lillie Mae Christopher.

I was filled with so much agony, to the point that my soul felt like it was coming apart. The pain and agony Jesus displayed in the Garden of Gethsemane before he was crucified immediately came to my mind. It was excruciating pain and suffering. I was silently screaming within my soul. But I had to keep it together for my family. My daughter had been my right arm with taking care of my mother.

Our family living situation changed after Adrienne died. My son moved to Vallejo, so he was too far away to assist me. My two grandchildren went to live with their father in Vegas. My mother and I remained together. Sadly, my mother did not grasp the idea that her road dog—her friend, and her only granddaughter—was dead. The dementia was taking a toll on her mind.

Thankfully, my mother did not try to cook, she was not violent, nor did she try to wander off again. Her daily routine was sitting in the kitchen chair, located by the window, and then back to her bed.

I made several attempts to hire someone to take care of my mother in the home while I was at work. I found good care providers, but they did not know how to relate to the stage of dementia my mother was dealing with. She would be aggressive with them. There were times when I returned home to find bruises on my mother. Enough was enough!

I quickly flushed the idea down the toilet of someone coming into our home to care for my mother. I moved on to Plan B.

So I could observe my mother while I was at work, I purchased an alarm system and had cameras stationed around the house. I was determined to make Plan B work.

My main goal was to keep my mother home with

me. I was in denial. Every day before I departed for work, I would change her pull-ups, dress her, and feed her breakfast. Then, put her back into bed, prepare her lunch, and put her food on the kitchen table with her favorite orange drink and cookies. After leaving, I would pray, and hope everything would be okay until I made it to work where I could watch her on the cameras, from my iPad.

One day, while at work watching her, I noticed her behavior was different. She did not get out of bed as usual. As I sat at my desk, I thought something must be wrong. Immediately I went home and observed her. I was led by the Holy Spirit to call the advice nurse. I had arranged for a transportation service through Kaiser to come and take her to the hospital.

It was New Year's Eve 2016, nearly three months after my daughter passed, that my mother was stricken with pneumonia and was hospitalized. I began to cry out to the Lord for strength and to heal my mother. He is certainly a present help in the time of need.

"I can do all things [which He has called me to do] through Him who strengthens and empowers me [to fulfill His purpose—I am self-sufficient in Christ's sufficiency; I am ready for anything and equal to anything through Him who infuses me with inner strength and confident peace]" (Philippians 4:13, AMP).

What a way to bring in the new year. My mother

remained in the hospital for two weeks. Her behavior was certainly not the norm. She was not in a familiar place, and sadly enough, the hospital staff did not seem to know how to deal with a person with full blown dementia. I had been caring for my mother for nearly eight years, but they refused to listen to my advice.

Whenever I was away from her bedside, I was told that my mother was combative with everyone. One day her hospital room was full of people observing her, and she could not handle it. Another time when I was away from her room, I was told she got out of bed and walked out the room with the back of her gown open, and feces all over her back and buttocks. She had a bowel movement in the bed and it was all over her. I am sure it was not a pretty sight.

When I returned to the hospital, a social worker met with me and asked tons of questions regarding my mother. She said, "Andrea, we know you are trying your hardest to take care of your mother by yourself and work a full-time job. We know you are doing the very best that you can. It would be best that you consider putting your mother into a care home."

The social worker immediately started going over the "what if's." The biggest "what if" was a scenario of my mother being home alone, and a fire breaks out, and her mind would not tell her to leave. She would just sit there. I could not live with the fact that something tragic happened to my mother while alone.

This made me feel as if I was sinking under a great deal of pressure. But I had to begin the search for a new home for my mother. It was one of the hardest and most agonizing decisions of my life.

On January 15, 2017, she was released from Kaiser. After her release, I was wracked with the thought of making the painful decision. In my mind I pondered, *What would people say or think of me?* I surrendered and placed my mother in a residential home for seniors.

During the first three weeks of living at home without my mother, I had countless sleepless nights. I was programmed to wake up in the middle of the night. My mother had a pattern: She would get out of bed in the middle of the night and walk to the kitchen to get lemon or vanilla cookies, located on the table. She would get the cookies, then return to her bed. I learned over time, this craving helped her with *sundowning*. Sundowning can cause a variety of behaviors: confusion, anxiety, aggression or ignoring directions, and pacing or wandering. Sundowning is not a disease, but a group of symptoms that occur at a specific time of the day or night; they may affect people with dementia, such as Alzheimer's disease.

After about six months, I realized and accepted the fact, it was safer for my mother to live in a residential home, and better for us as well. The monthly rate for her care would be roughly $3,000. I would not have to worry as much about my mother's welfare when I was not home. Nor would I have to be concerned about the big "What If!"

It would be a home away from home, always having a fresh atmosphere, and not that many residents. I started my mother out at a home licensed for twelve residents. Finally, I located a facility with six residents. It was operated by a Christian married couple with two care providers assisting them.

Now it was time for me to move to another location for a new beginning. On March 2, 2018, the Lord blessed me with a place to live in the same city as my mother, my son, and grandson. Thankfully, we live within walking distance to each other.

Sadly, my mother does not know my name anymore or that I am her daughter. Every time I go to visit her, it is so painful that I must leave her. The good news is that she is doing well with her health, still mobile, and holding on to her first name. Whenever I visit, I make it a point to give her some tender loving care, by hugging her and smothering her with tons of kisses on her cheek. I never leave without asking, "What's your name, Momma?" She always manages to say, "My name is Lillie."

I am the woman that I am today because of my mother's labors of love and her prayers. I am forever grateful for her love, her patience, and her many sacrifices for me (her only child) and her grand and great grandchildren. I am poring this love, this patience and many sacrifices on to my children and grandchildren. She taught and prepared me to never give up on my children or life, no matter how difficult the circumstances might appear to be. I must keep the faith and continue to trust God.

With the Love of God and a mother's love, nothing is impossible. The precious memories of my dear mother are engraved in my heart.

I have learned to treasure every moment that I spend with my mother. The experience of providing care for her over the years has stirred up the desire in me to open a residential home for seniors, specializing in dementia residents.

My mother's economic status is classified as middle class, due to her retirement benefits from the Postal Service. However, it is not enough money to meet the cost and necessities it takes for a person with dementia and living in a residential home. I am praying and preparing to open three residential homes for seniors who merely do not qualify for any services because of their income.

Thank you, Lord Jesus, for your divine strength to finish this journey with my incredible mother.

Thank you, Lillie Mae Christopher, for your strength, your courage, and your amazing love for your FAMILY.

What's your name, Momma? My name is Lillie!

"And we know that all things work together for good to them that love God, to them who are the called according to his purpose" (Romans 8:28, KJV).

About the Author

Andrea Mills is a published author of several books writing under her pen name, Michele Mills. An inspirational speaker, visionary, and entrepreneur, she is the Founder and CEO of Love In Spite of Women's Bible Fellowship, where Jesus Christ is Lord. Women's ministry leader and Bible teacher, in 2014, Andrea launched the 1st Annual Prophetic Women's Crusade, which was embraced by the mighty presence of the Holy Spirit, manifested through signs and wonders from God in Heaven.

Andrea resides in Northern California. The mother of two children., Adrienne, her late daughter, and a son, Andrè, She also has three grandchildren: Charnell, Ronal III, and Chase Benjamin.

For more information or to schedule for speaking engagement or book signing contact Michele_amills@yahoo.com

www.loveinspiteofwomensbiblefellowship.org

www.ingramcontent.com/pod-product-compliance
Lightning Source LLC
Chambersburg PA
CBHW071138090426
42736CB00012B/2158

* 9 7 8 0 9 8 9 9 9 6 9 1 9 2 *